life. after. theory

life. after. theory

edited by
Michael Payne
and
John Schad

continuum
LONDON • NEW YORK

Continuum

The Tower Building   15 East 26th Street
11 York Road   New York
London SE1 7NX   NY 10010

First published 2003 by Continuum
Paperback edition first published 2004 by Continuum

British Library Cataloguing-in-Publication Data
A catalogue record for this book is available from the British Library.

ISBN HB: 0–8264–6565–X
    PB: 0–8264–7317–2

Typeset by YHT Ltd, London
Printed and bound in Great Britain by MPG Books Ltd, Bodmin, Cornwall

contents

acknowledgements vi

preface: what are we after? ix

1 following theory: Jacques Derrida 1

2 value after theory: Frank Kermode 52

3 truth after theory: Christopher Norris 78

4 music, religion and art after theory:
Frank Kermode and Christopher Norris 115

5 feminist theory after theory: Toril Moi 133

epilogue: coming back to 'life': John Schad 168

notes 190

index 195

acknowledgements

We would like to thank all those who helped with the two 'life.after.theory' conferences at Loughborough University – very many colleagues and postgraduates in the Department of English and Drama helped in very many ways. We should, though, make particular mention of Pauline Higgs for her administration, Clare Hanson, Marion Shaw and Kevin Mills for their lifts, Dave Hill for his recording, Simon King, James Holden and Jessica Butt for their transcribing, and – above all – Jonathan Taylor for all his hard work. Finally, we would also like to thank Tristan Palmer for his unwavering commitment to the project.

Michael Payne
John Schad

All royalties from this book will go to Oxfam.

... *a criticism of life*. The end and aim of all literature, if one considers it attentively, is, in truth, nothing but that.

Matthew Arnold, 'Joubert'

If death is not opposable it is, already, *life death.*

Jacques Derrida, *The Post Card*

CLOV: Do you believe in the life to come?
HAMM: Mine was always that.

Samuel Beckett, *Endgame*

A good book is the precious life-blood of a master-spirit, embalmed and treasured up on purpose to a life beyond life.

John Milton, *Aeropagitica*

It's life and life only.

Bob Dylan, 'It's Alright Ma'

... that hateful mystification known as 'life'.

Simone de Beauvior, *The Prime of Life*

... there is life and life.

Henry James, Preface to *The Tragic Muse*

preface

what are we after?

John Schad

> Philosophy always comes on the scene too late.... As the
> *thought* of the world, it appears only when actuality is
> already there, cut and dried.... It is only with the fall of dusk
> that the owl of Minerva spreads its wings.
> Hegel, Philosophy of Right

For those of us within the small world of academic literary studies it seems that philosophy has come not too
late but too early – literary theory, 'the *thought* of' our
world, seems to have come and gone, the moment of
'high' theory appears to have passed. 'Theory', of course,
is a notoriously loose term, covering as it does a whole
multitude of critical and intellectual sins most of which
have been committed in the name of 'poststructuralism'
which is itself a loose term including, among other
things, such diverse developments as Lacanian psychoanalysis, Kristevan feminism, Althusserian Marxism,
Derridean deconstruction and Foucaldian history. In one
such form or another poststructuralism got almost
everywhere; if it can be said (speaking very roughly) to
have begun in Paris in the late 1960s, and peaked in Yale
in the 1970s and 1980s, then it has been busy declining
in a university 'near you' in the second half of the

nineties. Indeed, in the last few years there have been a number of books marking this passing – witness, for example, Thomas Docherty's *After Theory* (1996), Wendell Harris's *Beyond Poststructuralism* (1996) and Martin McQuillan's *Post-Theory* (1999). Some, in such books, have argued that theory has been discredited; some that it has simply grown old and outdated; some that it has completed its task, that theory has now vanished into new, and better critical practice; others that it is impossible to talk of the end of a body of thought that itself does so much to problematize notions of historical linearity. In addition, there are those who point out that the word 'after' can mean not only 'following in time' but also 'in pursuit of' or even 'in imitation of'. *Could* life be in pursuit of theory? *Could* life ever imitate theory? And, indeed, what is 'life'? Whatever the answer to that, whatever story we tell of the last thirty years, and whatever way(s) you read 'after', there *is* a widespread understanding, explicit or implicit, that literary studies is now experiencing something we might just call 'life after theory'.

What follows is an attempt to respond to both this phrase and the 'event' it seems to describe. To do this we have brought together four of the scholars who have been most influential both in and 'after' theory: namely, Jacques Derrida, Frank Kermode, Christopher Norris and Toril Moi. Each contributes an interview held at some point between November 2001 and July 2002, either at Loughborough University in the UK or Duke University in the USA. In the case of Kermode, Norris and Moi – all of whom were interviewed by Michael Payne – it was a case of life (or theory) repeating itself since Mike first interviewed them at Bucknell University in the USA as part of a series of events that were subsequently published as the *Bucknell Theory Lectures* (Blackwell, 1990–4).

Exactly what is happening in these interviews is something that I attempt to explore in the Epilogue, but in the meantime we leave it to readers to decide for themselves – to decide, for instance, whether the owl of Minerva, the bird of theory, is finally shot; whether it is now worn like a dead albatross; or whether it makes one last, belated and glorious flight. Whatever, it is our hope that the book will both reflect upon life after theory and actively explore and enact what that might yet be or mean for critic, text and, indeed, world – or, if you will, 'Life'. (Did someone say 'Leavis'?)

1

following theory
Jacques Derrida

BIOGRAPHICAL NOTE by James Holden

For more than thirty-five years, Jacques Derrida has been preeminent in the Humanities. Always a controversial figure, his expansive and notoriously complex *œuvre* has been both celebrated and denounced; for many he has become one of the major figures in Western philosophy, for some he is an 'embarrassment' whose writing 'defies comprehension'.

Born in Algeria in 1930 to a Sephardic Jewish family, Derrida did not move to France until 1949 where he progressed, sometimes haltingly, towards a career in academic philosophy. In 1964, after four years at the Sorbonne, Derrida moved to the École Normale Supérieure, where he remained for twenty years. It was, though, as early as 1966 that Derrida arrived on the international scene with his seminal lecture 'Structure, Sign and Play' which was given at a now-famous colloquium at Johns Hopkins University, Baltimore; a year later Derrida published *Of Grammatology*, a 'book' which opens by announcing 'The End of the Book and the Beginning of Writing'. Since 1984 Derrida has worked at the École des Hautes Études en Sciences Sociales, while also being a Visiting Professor at both Yale and California, Irvine. In 1992 Derrida was, after much controversy, awarded an honorary doctorate by Cambridge University. This controversy took the form of a very public debate regarding his right to such an award, with nineteen Cambridge dons writing to *The Times* to denounce Derrida's work. The issue was finally put to a vote, the first of its kind in almost thirty years; the pro-Derrida lobby triumphed by 336 votes to 204.

This vote did not, though, signal a simple assimilation of Derrida's work, which continues to have a complex relationship to the academy and, in particular, that key institution of the academy, the institution of philosophy. As Derrida remarks, 'the task of deconstruction' is 'to discover the non-place ... which would be the "other" of philosophy'. Derrida's exploration of this 'non-place' has involved him in extraordinarily close-reading of not only the great canon of philosophy – thinkers such as Plato, Kant, Hegel and Husserl – but also a great deal of writing usually thought of as literary: witness his engagement with writers such as Kafka, Joyce, Celan and Blanchot. The astonishing range of Derrida's reading is, perhaps, matched only by the range of his concerns; as Derrida once remarked, 'deconstructive work addresses [not only] ... the theme of crisis or critique, but also – [and] the list is unending – that of science, truth, literature, politics, sexual difference, the democracy to come, [and] the Enlightenment of today and tomorrow.' To read Derrida is, then, to be, like Derrida himself, 'constantly surprised ... [and] having a feeling of being always on the verge.' At the same time one also has a sense of quite remarkable consistency, of a sustained, rigorous and even ethical commitment to the other. To quote Derrida, 'deconstruction is ... a positive response to an alterity which necessarily calls, summons, or motivates it. Deconstruction is therefore vocation – a response to a call.'

EDITORIAL NOTE ─────────

On the afternoon of 10 November 2001, Jacques Derrida participated in a round-table discussion which constituted the first of the two 'life.after.theory' events held in the Department of English and Drama at Loughborough University. Professor Derrida responded to questions put to him by Professor Nicholas Royle, Professor Christopher Norris and Dr Sarah Wood, all of whom have published extensively on deconstruction. Derrida also responded to some questions from the audience. In all, Derrida spoke for almost two hours, without any notes and in English. He modestly asked the audience to forgive him for his English, and would like that request to be echoed here. It should also be remembered that this text is not, of course, something Derrida has written, but rather a transcript of an astonishing oral performance.

This performance followed a lecture by Derrida in the morning. The lecture was entitled 'Perjuries' and itself arose out of a strange, almost uncanny moment in Derrida's own life – as Derrida himself explained in the lecture:

> Toward the end of the 1970s, at Yale, [my friend] Paul de Man said to me one day something like this:
> > If you want to know a part of my life, read 'Hölderlin en Amérique.' Henri Thomas, whom I knew here, in America after the war, published this text in *Mercure de France*, and it was reprinted [in 1964] . . . as a novel [called] . . . *Le parjure*.
> I confess that I did not rush out looking for the book . . . . Years

3

later, at a bookseller's in Nice, where I was on vacation, I came upon *Le parjure*. I read it very quickly, but very quickly understood that the principal character ... Stéphane Chalier, resembled in certain features the real person of Paul de Man; [the novel told] the story of a second marriage, in the United States, while a first marriage in Europe had not ended in legal divorce. Hence the accusation of bigamy and perjury .... After my reading I remember that I wrote to Paul de Man, a few words, as discreetly as possible, in conformity with the customary tone of our exchanges, saying that I had been *bouleversé*, bowled over. We never spoke about it again; just as I never spoke about it with Henri Thomas whom I didn't know at the time and whom I nevertheless telephoned, years later, in 1987 ... to hear his response to what ... had just [been] discovered about the past ... of Paul de Man.

What had just been discovered was that between 1940 and 1942, during the Nazi occupation of Belgium, Paul de Man had written a series of articles for two collaborationist newspapers. After the war de Man, of course, had moved to America and become a leading figure in what was known as 'the Yale school of deconstruction'. The parallels between Paul de Man and Stéphane Chalier, the *fictional* Belgian in America with the secret past, are obvious and provide one crucial point of reference throughout the round-table discussion. Equally important is Stéphane's haunting response to the accusation of perjury: 'Just imagine, I was not thinking about it.'[1] It is with precisely these words that Derrida began his lecture, and for Derrida they raised a number of questions – most obviously, the question of *not* thinking and what that might mean for the Cartesian notion of a continuous thinking self; this led Derrida to the more general questions of continuity and discontinuity, sequence and consequence – or, more specifically, what does or does not *follow*. This, in turn, shaded into discussion of *who* does or does not follow, a discussion that focused on two particular figures: the person of the acolyte (literally, 'a follower,' from the Greek word *akolouthos*) and the rhetorical device known as anacoluthon, which the dictionary defines as 'a sentence or construction lacking grammatical sequence'. It is with these two figures that Nick Royle begins the round table.

Nicholas Royle: The first question that I would like to ask is, I suppose, a question in three parts and it's about the acolyte and anacoluthon. The acolyte is the follower and thus is the apparent opposite of anacoluthon. Anacoluthon is what fails to follow; it's what's non-sequential or literally 'without following' (*an*, privative, *akolouthos*, 'following'). So I thought with this question about the acolyte and anacoluthon I could take anacoluthon first, seeing as it's second, and ask whether we could read 'life.after.theory' as an anacoluthon. I think I'll just leave that as the first part of the question.

The second is this: Jacques, I wonder if you would be kind enough to say something about the figure of the acolyte? In particular, I was thinking of the sense that, following your work, the notion of the follower or acolyte becomes difficult, indeed perhaps impossible. 'Who follows another follows nothing' is a quotation from Montaigne, which we might relate to something that you say in *Monolingualism of the Other*: 'Contrary to what one is often most tempted to believe, the master is nothing.' So, I wonder if you might say a little bit more about the notion of the acolyte, given that it seems to me in many ways inappropriate, perhaps impossible, to think of you as the acolyte of, let's say, Foucault or Freud or Heidegger. I wonder if this is partly because, without wishing to understate the importance of notions of fidelity that I think pervade everything that you write, it is difficult not to feel that your signature or the singularity of your work has to do with the figure of the anacoluthon about which you were speaking earlier.

The third part of this question has to do with the idea that one cannot follow the figure of the anacoluthon in your work *without* following, *without* grammar, *without* a fidelity to grammar. This third part of the question has to do, in particular, with the figure of the woman. I'm struck by the way in which woman seems to figure as a kind of anacoluthon in a number of your texts. I'm thinking, for example, of the end of *Otobiographies* where you say, apropos of Nietzsche's lectures on the future of our educational institutions, 'Woman never appears at any point along the umbilical cord, either to study or to teach, no woman or trace of woman'; or, at the end of 'Step of Hospitality/No Hospitality' [*Pas d'hospitalité*], where you are speaking of, precisely, the end of the story (in Judges 19) and you remark: 'In the name of hospitality, all the men are *sent* a woman, to be precise, a concubine'; or, at the end of this morning's lecture, where you spoke of what you call a kind of idiocy of man, finally focusing on the figure of 'an impassive and, at bottom, inaccessible woman'. In each case, woman comes, in a sense, to surprise or anacoluthize (if I can say that) everything you've been saying.

At issue here is perhaps a broader 'question of style', as you pose it in *Éperons.* I wonder if you can say a little bit more about this grammaticality or a-grammaticality of the woman and about the way in which she seems to turn up at the end of these texts. Linked to this, I wonder if you could perhaps elaborate a little more on the relation or non-relation between the woman and the acolyte.

Jacques Derrida: Thank you, Nick, you've said a lot of things already. It is not a question, it's already a set of original propositions. Now, to formalize everything I will try to say, I would say – in the most formalized form – of the logic which was at work in my lecture, in fact in your questions too, that there is no simple opposition between the acolyte, or the 'acoluthon' and the '*ana*coluthon'. That is a problem, because to accompany, or to follow in the most demanding and authentic way, implies the '*ana*col,' the 'not-following,' the break in the following, in the company so to speak. So, if we agree on this, a number of consequences will follow: you cannot simply oppose the acolyte and the anacoluthon – logically they are opposed; but in fact, what appears as a necessity is that, in order to follow in a consistent way, to be true to what you follow, you have to interrupt the following. So, let me leave this statement in its abstract form and then I would like to go back to the series of questions that you ask.

'Life.after.theory'; I'm not sure, from the very beginning, that I understood what this title meant, the 'after'. To 'be after' may mean that you try and be consistent with what you left, you try to live after theory in a way which is consistent with theory, what you have said in theory; *or*, if you survive theory, you do something else. So, this is the opposition. 'After' means 'according to' theory *or* simply *after* theory, breaking with theory as if life was something irreducible to theory. Now, I never use the word 'theory' in the way that you do here; I don't use the word 'theory' after you, after the Americans and the English speakers. So, I would translate this into French as 'life after philosophy', after deconstruction, after literature and so on and so forth. So, in that case, I try, I would say, in principle, to live my life *after* all these things by trying to be consistent with what I say, or what I write, or what I teach as a philosopher, as a deconstructive philosopher without making my life a simple application or consequence of what I say. My life is irreducible to what I say and it is certainly the case in, for instance, *The Post Card,* that I confess that everything I oppose, so to speak, in my texts, everything that I deconstruct – presence, voice, living, voice and so on – is exactly what I'm after in life. I love the voice, I love presence, I love ...; there is no love, no desire without it. So, I'm constantly denying, so to speak, in my life what I'm saying in my books or my teaching. Which doesn't mean that I don't believe what I write, but I try to understand why there is what I call Necessity, and I write this with a capital 'N' – Necessity, as if it were someone, perhaps a woman, a Necessity which compels me to say that there is no immediate presence, compels me to deconstruct and say that there *is* an interruption, there *is* a possibility for a letter not to arrive at its destination and so on ... . I take into account this Necessity and I obey, I account for, this Necessity. Nevertheless, in my life, I do the opposite. I live as if, as if it *were* possible for the letter to reach its destination or somehow to be present with voice, or vocal presence. I want to be close to my friends and to meet them and, if I don't, I use the phone. That's life, consistent with and inconsistent with, following without following. But, I'm trained to think: 'What's going on? Why do I insist on the fact that there is no pure presence?' And nevertheless, nevertheless, because, because there is no such thing, because there is this Necessity, it is because of that that there is a desire for presence and intimacy. So, I try to articulate the Necessity which urges me, compels me to write and to teach what I write, and this articulation means that it's *because* there is no pure presence that I desire it. There would be no desire without it. So I try to articulate, to articulate this consistency and *in*consistency. In this respect, the word 'after' may move around a double meaning: 'after' as in coming after, or 'post'; and 'after' in the sense of 'according to' – *d'après* ... following without following.

The second question. I often repeat that my relation to the masters that you mentioned – Freud, Heidegger – is a relation of fidelity and betrayal; and I betray them because I want to be true to them. In reading Freud and many others I try not to betray them; I try to understand what they mean and to do justice to what they write and to follow, to follow them as far as possible and as closely as possible, up to a certain point. When I say 'up to a certain point' I mean that there is a moment that I betray them. *Within* the experience of following them there is something other, something new, or something different which occurs and which I sign. That's what I call a 'counter-sign', a counter-signature, a term I use very often. A counter-signature is a signature which both confirms the first signature, the former signature, and nevertheless is opposed to it; and in any case it's new, it's my *own* signature. A counter-signature is this strange alliance between following and not following, confirming and displacing; and displacing is the only way to pay homage, to do justice. If I just repeat, if I interpret 'following' as just repetition, following in a way, in a mechanical way, just repeating, not animating, it's another way of betraying. So, if I want to follow, I have to hear. In French we say *écouter*, to listen to *and* at the same time to hear, to understand, to do our best to understand, and to obey at the same time. If I want to listen to the teachings of Freud, Heidegger and others there is a point at which in order to listen to what they say or write I have to say something, I have to say something, not simply to take but, rather, to write in my turn. And when I write I say something else, there is something new, something different and that's the way I understand fidelity; this is fidelity in theory, in philosophy, in literature; this is fidelity in everyday life – in marriage, for instance. You cannot simply repeat the same thing, you have to invent, to do something else if only to respect the alterity of the other.

I understand that the question of the marriage vows was, this morning, considered interesting by some of you, the 'yes' to the marriage, the performative 'yes' – 'I do', 'I do'. This 'yes' has to be repeated differently each time. If it's simply a record saying 'I do' 'I do' 'I do' there is no fidelity. For this 'I do' to be a renewed promise it has to be different each time, the same one and different. In order to follow the 'I do' today (before the priest), the 'I do' of tomorrow should be the same and different. They must follow one another and confirm themselves but, at the same time, be different. That's what the counter-signature is. Of course, even if I say to the same person 'I do' tomorrow and after tomorrow, the fact that this 'I do' is different, to some extent, means at the same time fidelity and betrayal. Indeed, it's a kind of perjury to say 'I do' to someone. So that may be the paradox in the twin concepts of *acoluthia* and ana-coluthon. You have to betray in order to be truthful. That's why in theoretical texts, other than the one that I delivered this morning, I try to show that perjury is not simply the betrayal of an oath. There is a perjury at the very beginning of the promise. It is impossible to avoid perjury, and I have tried to show this in the context of a reading of Levinas. I have already betrayed Levinas in order to be faithful to him. Levinas said, for instance, that the ethical relation is a face-to-face relation, a dual relation: I'm facing the Other, respecting the Other and being responsible to the Other, for the Other – there are two. But, admittedly, he has to add 'what about the third one, the third party?' And he says, 'Well for justice to appear a third party must be part of the dual rela-tion.' As soon as there is a third party there is another Other; and this third party is included in the dual rela-tion from the very beginning, if only because I speak, and when one speaks there are more than two. If the third party that is justice is involved in the dual relationship then I must, necessarily, betray the Other. I owe my respect, my love, my fidelity to this one and nevertheless, as soon as I speak, I include a third one in the relationship and this is already a perjury. The perjury is part of the process. It is not simply an accident which corrupts the promise, it's *part* of the promise. So you cannot call perjury a 'quasi-transcendental perjury'. Perjury is part of it, part of fidelity. That may sound paradoxical, or tragic but I think this is necessity; of necessity you can't avoid perjury. This means that the *acoluthia* and the analocuthon are not opposed.

Now, the third part of your remarks, about the woman. Yes, in a certain way, the woman in many texts of mine represents precisely the absolute Other; not because it is more other than the others, the other others, but because in our culture, in what prevails in our culture, the woman is, so to speak, excluded or in an asymmetrical relationship. She represents precisely the one who is outside of the system, excluded from the system; and, being excluded from the system, the woman represents this excess, this break, this absolute transcendence. Not that I think that this is *essentially* the case, but in 'our' culture (forgive me, not just 'our' culture but almost everywhere in the world) the woman represents the figure of the absolute Other and so I try, in many dialogical texts – or texts in which there are not simply two but more than one voice – I try to embody this absolute Other in the feminine voice. That is also a strategy. But I wouldn't speak of some a-grammaticality of the woman. Of course, each time there is this break in the following, this inconsistency, this interruption, there is some a-grammaticality – that was part of your second question. Even when we want to *break* with the discourse, or logic, or grammar – that is, to reach a point of a-grammaticality – we have to *follow* the grammar. That is what I try to do when I read a text. Even when, as I said at the beginning, I try to locate an interruption, a break, an inconsistency, or some inarticulation, I have, in order to locate this, to think of this, I have to respect the grammar. I have to know the language. I cannot deconstruct Heidegger if I don't read Heidegger, if I don't read German, if I don't respect the grammaticality of the discourse. But again, there is no opposition between grammaticality and some a-grammaticality, and in the case of the woman I wouldn't say that the woman represents some ungrammaticality. If in these contexts it represents a force of resistance which resists the authority of a given grammar, it will *dis*organize but not as something absolutely wild but as some other force which compels us to write differently, to organize society differently. It is another force which sometimes takes the form of a-grammaticality. There is no pure a-grammaticality; or rather, there *is* pure a-grammaticality but as soon as it appears as such, or as it enters a text or a situation, it starts to become grammatical. That's why the transaction is required, why every text is a transaction between a given set of grammatical rules, and this is the case in literature, philosophy and even in everyday language. In short, there is both a given set of hegemonic grammatical rules *and* something which looks a-grammatical, which pushes or transforms the given power. Then there is a transformation of the grammar itself. What we do when we do something, when we write, when we use grammar is invent new grammatical rules which in their turn will be challenged. An event is not simply an interruption, a break in the rules, in what is predictable, it's already the production of new rules, a new expression, a new text.

Let me just add something which has to do with the language: 'to follow' in French is *suivre* and when I say 'I follow' in French, I say *je suis* which also means 'I am' so it complicates, it complicates the grammar.

Sarah Wood: In *Le parjure*, the novel you discussed this morning, when Stéphane Chalier asks the narrator for a report-confession – 'you will write it, won't you?' – we are told that these words are spoken in anger, and that is what I wanted to ask you about. I wanted to ask about anger. 'He spoke in anger and did not remember when I reminded him of it.' In your lecture you return to – and just now it seems to me you've also spoken about – an irreducible distraction in the heart of finite thought. I would associate this with forgetting, and in the lines I've just quoted it's associated with speaking in anger. I've noticed that your work sometimes makes people very angry. I've also noticed that you speak in a friendly way, there's a lot of warmth and patience; but I wanted to ask you this question. I also wanted to associate with it what you were saying this morning about 'the twilight' which is introduced by the identifications in the novel and which, perhaps, makes all the figures in it and the reader of it somewhat ghostly – makes us look like ghosts, makes us ghosts. The question is not in my own words, it comes from Robert Browning – it's also a ghost question: 'why should ghosts feel angered?'[2]

Jacques Derrida: Ghosts? The anger of ghosts – I believe there is such an anger, if only in ourselves, and it's the most terrible anger because we cannot respond, or they cannot respond to our response. Let me say first that when I referred to the woman in the novel, and said she was outside the dual, all-male relationship, I was just commenting on the grammar of the text, it is *in the text*; it was not my thesis, I was just reading it. It is the narrator who says, addressing the woman, that 'we're sleeping we, two men, like idiots, and you were mastering everything and you were making decisions'. That's a masculine reproach, it's the narrator's discourse. He's a man. I tried not to erase the fact that they were two male friends, and this goes back to something I wrote in another context – *The Politics of Friendship* – about friendship between two men, the woman being excluded from the history of friendship. That is what I had in mind.

As for this morning's discussion of the problem of finitude, well it is *because* we are finite beings that forgetting, or distraction is irreducible in a certain way; but it is also because of finitude that we need oath and fidelity – it is precisely because there *is* this amnesia, this possible, always possible, destruction or amnesia. Otherwise we wouldn't need oaths and fidelity. This means that finitude produces at the same time both the possibility of evil – that is, destruction, amnesia and infidelity – *and* the urge for fidelity. It is the same system. An infinite being cannot forget, and for that very reason doesn't have to promise anything. The promise itself attests to the fact that we are finite, that we may forget; which means that the possibility of evil is *part* of the opposite – again, *acoluthia* and anacoluthon.

Now for the anger about which you asked. When, in *Le parjure*, Stéphane asks the narrator to write the report *in his place*, not only the report but the confession – writing a report is easier because it just has to tell the story as objective story – it means that he signs a self-accusation. To sign a *report* for another is not the same thing as to sign a *confession* for another. So when Stéphane asks the narrator to sign, or countersign a report-confession (in a single word with a hyphen: 'report-confession') the explosion of anger is the resistance to this impossible injunction that the narrator, nevertheless, accepts. He says 'Yes, I have to do this out of friendship, I owe him this. I think he lied, he is a perjurer, he is guilty; nevertheless, out of friendship, I'm going to be on his side.' He accepts the injunction and at the same time he refuses, he becomes angry: 'Why me? Why should I do that?' His anger is the sign and the symptom of this double bind.

To go back to your reference to the ghost, we have to do with ghosts here because, first of all, the narrator, as a narrator, is a survivor; because, when you tell a story, especially when you sign a confession, you already write something which in principle might survive. The story, and the true subject of the story – *and* the book now, because the two men are dead – is a survivor. It is a ghost story in a certain way. When I say this I am speaking as the ghost of Paul de Man, as the ghost of Henri Thomas. Now, anger is always the anger of ghosts because when we get angry it means, at least among other things, that we to some extent identify precisely with the one we're angry at; otherwise I wouldn't be angry. The narrator becomes angry because he identified with the other, with Stéphane; otherwise he would say: 'No, I won't sign this confession. I'm not interested.' He becomes angry because he feels that he will have to do what he doesn't want to do and he is caught up in this double bind. He is not what he is, he is not who he is, and that's why the spectral, or spectrality enters the scene.

You also asked me, in a personal way, why people are angry at me. To a large extent I don't know. It's up to them to answer. To some small extent I know; it is not usually because people are angry at me personally (well, it happens in private, perhaps); but rather they are angry at what I *write*. They are angry at my texts more than anything else, and I think it is because of the *way* I write – not the content, or the thesis. They say that I do not obey the usual rules of rhetoric, grammar, demonstration and argumentation; but, of course, if they were simply not interested, they would not be angry. As it is, they start to get involved but feel that it's not that easy, that to read my texts they have to change the rules, to read differently, if only at another rhythm. They have to change the way they usually read and that's why they get angry; not because they are charging me with saying terrible things, I don't think. Sometimes they allege that what I'm saying is outrageous but I don't think that this is the real reason why they get angry. It is because I write differently. Well, I respect grammar. You cannot, I hope, find anything a-grammatical, anything wrong according to grammar, in my texts; but there is, sometimes, undecidability, many ways of hearing and under-standing a sentence – as, for instance, when I said, a moment ago, 'between anacoluthon and *acoluthon* there is no opposition' or 'when I promise I perjure already'. It all makes *me* angry. But that's Necessity.

Now, just one more word abut the ghost. I tried, of course, to pay attention to the generality of this spec-trality – there is spectrality everywhere. So the ghost, which is neither present or absent, neither alive nor dead, is everywhere – *as is the anger.* That's why I think being angry is not a bad way of reading; being angry is always a reaction to some spectrality of the text and some spectral reaction. The one who is angry cannot be one with what he or she is; there is a split, there is a double bind in anger. When you are angry you are in some senses pretending to be angry and you are a split subject. So, there is some ghostly dimension in anger as is the case in so many other experiences.

Christopher Norris: One person, one philosopher, who famously got very angry with you was John Searle. I guess that, had he been at the lecture this morning, he would probably have been angry again, and for some of the same reasons. He would probably have said:

> Here we have Derrida once again mixing things up by con-
> fusing the orders of normal (straightforward, felicitous,
> everyday) speech-acts and deviant, for instance, fictive, but
> also – in the strange case you've been discussing – retro-
> actively efficacious speech-acts.

He would have said (I guess) that in fact we have a
perfectly good working grasp of such distinctions, no
doubt one that is mostly applied in a tacit, unconscious,
pre-theoretical kind of way and that requires working
out in more detail by philosophers but still a perfectly
adequate working grasp. Elsewhere in his writing, when
he talks about the 'problem' of fictional reference,
Searle takes a similar commonsense line: that we can
and do distinguish clearly enough between normal,
everyday assertoric uses of language (where truth-values
apply, since referring expressions are taken to 'go
through' in the usual way) and fictive uses of language
where those values are of course suspended, since fictional 'referents' belong to a realm of inexistent pseudo-
entities that clearly cannot play such a role. And, for
Searle, fictive language is by definition, of its very nature, a non-standard kind of language that we recognize
as non-standard and for which we make special allow-
ances – poetic licence or whatever. This is pretty much
the standard attitude among most analytic philosophers
of language. It is the kind of argument you find in Frege's essay 'On Sense and Reference' where he argues
that sense determines reference (that is to say, we pick
out objects and persons by applying some range of
predicates or descriptive attributes) but also that, in
normal cases, the reference has to go through – and

designate some real-world existent object or person – if the statement is to count as a genuine (truth-apt) assertion. So in the case of fictive utterances such as 'Odysseus stepped ashore at Ithaca' we can say that they possess sense all right, that they are intelligible on their own (fictive or poetic) terms, but they don't go through in the normal way and are therefore simply not up for assessment as true or false. And of course there was Russell's famous 'Theory of Descriptions', developed at about the same time, which went a different but closely related way around in trying to resolve the problem about fictive reference.

Now, I've always thought that your work raises all kinds of fascinating, complex, intriguing questions about reference. You've very often been misunderstood as saying that 'there's no such thing as the referential dimension of language', or 'there's nothing outside the text'. There's a notorious sort of simplistic, naive mis-reading of your statement '*il n'y a pas de hors-texte*' which says that you're some kind of transcendental idealist who doesn't believe that there's any reality beyond language or the play of textual representations. I think we can discount those vulgar misreadings, espe-cially after what we heard this morning. But it did strike me that there was some tension between, on the one hand, your repeated insistence that we're dealing here with a fiction – this is a novel, it's clearly designated as such on its cover and we mustn't be too quick to read all kinds of real-world analogies or correspondences into the text – and, on the other, your reiterated point that the various narrative tropes and allusions *do* have an extra-textual dimension, that they *don't* belong to some purely fictive (non-referential) domain. They stray across, as it were, and allude obliquely to the reality of certain historical and biographical events that have loomed very large in recent debate about Paul de Man's life and work. You're certainly trying to complicate the terms of any straightforward, 'commonsense' distinction between fictive and referential language, let's say, or at least what a philosopher like Searle would understand as referential language.

Still, I think you're very keen *not* to be understood as saying that we can simply collapse the distinction between fictive narrative and historical narrative as if history could be treated – on a par with fiction – as *nothing more* than a textual or rhetorical construct. You're not an out-and-out 'textualist' or a 'strong' constructivist in the sense of arguing, as some post-modern historiographers argue, that in the end there is no difference – no difference in referential status – between historical narrative and fictive narrative since they can't be distinguished through the kinds of textual analysis that focus on matters of narrative emplotment, rhetorical structure, discursive representation and so forth. In fact you've always been careful to say – especially in recent interviews – that you don't *deny* or *reject* the idea of reference but have rather sought to 'complicate' or 'refine' it, to point out certain problems with standard (e.g., Searlean) ways of treating the referential function of language. But I wonder about what you were claiming this morning with regard to the relationship between Henri Thomas's novel – its fictive representation of certain events – and what we know, or think we know, or can (perhaps) reasonably surmise about certain much-discussed episodes in the life of Paul de Man.

Of course this whole question is further complicated by the extent to which de Man himself famously (or notoriously) problematized the concept of historical truth, and above all that of confessional truth – the idea of accurate, honest self-reckoning in the form of confessional narrative. His critics and detractors have been very keen to pick up on that. Thus they have said that de Man's entire project was devoted to inventing various 'textualist' strategies in order to dissimulate his guilty secret, to cover his tracks by making the case – as in his essay on Rousseau – that any attempt honestly to confess the events of one's own life was simply a form of narrative 'excuse' or self-exculpating fictive construction. So we are supposed to think that his deconstructive readings of Rousseau, Nietzsche, Proust and others amount to no more than a crafty means of evading responsibility for what he'd once written. Now of course that's a very crude kind of approach and there are other readings of his work – your own among them – that are both more adequate in textual-interpretative terms and more sensitive to the moral and political issues involved. But there is still this nagging problem, I think, that in de Man's work, and in Hillis Miller's also, one finds statements to the effect that the ethical moment in reading – in reading *any* kind of text, not only fictive texts – is first and foremost one that results from a certain linguistic predicament, described by Miller (in distinctly de Manian terms) as the 'structural interference of two linguistic codes'. Such statements can very easily be taken to espouse an extreme textualist or anti-realist position which denies the reality of past events (i.e., the belief that we can make true or false statements concerning them), which rejects the concept of truthfulness or good faith as applied to first-person (autobiographical) discourse, and which thus leaves no room for any notion of our having or taking present responsibility for past deeds or words.

This connects in turn with the question of selfhood or personhood, the continuity of personal identity across time, which you raised in your lecture this morning. It also connects with certain issues you have addressed in the context of Austinian speech-act philosophy, which takes us back to that exchange with John Searle. Thus it is a matter of asking: are we always bound to keep promises or to honour commitments (marriage vows, in the case of de Man) that were perhaps entered into under circumstances so remote from our present situation that we are apt to say: 'I am a different person now and that vow is no longer binding'? Or again, what precisely is the ethical obligation that requires us to be truthful when recounting episodes from our past life, episodes which – as de Man is at pains to demonstrate – may always turn out to elude our best efforts of memorial reconstruction? Then there is the issue (according to Searle, a non-issue) of whether we can possibly lay down criteria for distinguishing 'genuine', good-faith performatives from those that are 'deviant', 'parasitical', 'etiolated', or otherwise – as in the case of fictional performatives – devoid of 'serious' force. Here also it is a matter of sincerity-conditions, of meaning what one says – in the supposed standard case – and of somehow being held to that original meaning (whether by law, social convention or moral conscience) despite any intervening lapse of time or change of personal circumstance.

Hence my point – or rather your point in this morning's lecture – about personal identity and just what it is that leads us to think of ourselves and others as unique individuals who persist across time and who *do* have some special responsibility for our own words and actions past, present and future. Some of your remarks seemed to imply that the self is radically discontinuous, almost in the way that Hume maintained – namely, that personal identity is a form of illusion, that there is no 'deep further fact' about the self, and that when we look inward and try to discover it we find nothing more than a bundle of fleeting sensory impressions, memories, anticipations and so forth. So, what we think of as 'the self' is, in fact, a fictive construct or set of social (among them, legal or contractual) conventions that we have to abide by simply in order to maintain any kind of civilized coexistence. I wonder whether you'd accept that characterization which, after all, is the upshot of Hume's radical empiricism. Or would you accept any version of the Kantian claim that in order to make sense of such ideas as selfhood or moral obligation we must have recourse to some 'deep further fact', one that can only be established by means of transcendental (or conditions-of-possibility) arguments?

Jacques Derrida: Thank you. These are very difficult questions. Let me start right at the end with the last part of your question. Of course, when I pay attention to the possible breaks in identity I don't mean that we should not reaffirm, *as much as possible,* the identity, the self-identity which is the condition of responsibility and so on and so forth. Nevertheless, this phenomenon 'I think' – this 'I am the same' – is not something natural or given. It is precisely the product of the oath, or the product of the commitment, and it is a stabilized artefact; and '*we*' as a society need such artefacts – such reliable, stable, civilized identities; they are very strong. They are, though, historical, not purely transcendental; they are constituted through histories, long ones, even among animals, and each of these histories is different. So, I would interpret identity as an artefact that I take very seriously, while trying to avoid its naturalization or even ontologization. This means that there *is* no identity, there is only identification or self-identification *as a process*; and, indeed, that there *is* stabilization of identity only means or confirms that there can be a break, there can be pathology, there can be ruptures. The two go together. It is *because* the break is always possible that we need and perform identification, and society is organized according to this production of artefacts. I have nothing against this. However, when I realize that the production of these identifications is dangerous or one has some political or ethical reason to reproach this production, then I struggle. And I am the product of this struggle, which might be a political struggle against some identification – national identification, to start with.

It's a political struggle, and I can't fight precisely because I know that this identification is not natural – that, for instance, national identification is a historical product that can be deconstructed, or analysed, and which is always fragile. Even if it is very strong, the strength attests to the fragility. It is because it is fragile that it is so strong. So that's where the struggle and even deconstruction stops.

Now, in my own case – I mean, theoretically – I have *tried,* the best I could, to avoid being inconsistent; I try to write and to say and to teach in a certain way which prevents me, as much as possible, from, let's say, contradicting myself or changing. I try. Even if I think, 'Well, there *are* contradictions or aporias in my own texts', it is because I'm saying things which *are* self-contradicting or aporetic; so, *I point to them* and I try to formalize the aporia or the self-contradiction in order not to be inconsistent, not to say, 'Well, that is what I wrote when I was 25.' I try not to. And I would be presumptuous enough to say that you couldn't find discontinuity in my theoretical discourse. There are a lot of changes in terms of emphasis, or displacements, but there is no systemic discontinuity. So I try to assume my own theoretical signatures, as much as possible.

Now, going back to your first questions. You're right, in the debates I had with Searle and others the question of literature was, indeed, central. Of course, I never ever denied that we have to pay attention to everyday language, and the way reference works in everyday language. I have nothing against this, but at some point I tried to argue *against,* not speech-act theory in general, but some of Searle's statements, that, first of all, fictionality might be part, structurally, of everyday language. If you don't integrate the possibility of fiction in the most serious statement – the 'I do' is always the example – and if you don't take into account the possibility for this 'I promise' to be a lie or a fiction or literature, then you don't understand everyday language itself. So that's why I paid such attention to literature this morning.

Of course, referentiality is not simply part of everyday, serious language; there is also referentiality in fiction, even though it is a *different kind* of referentiality. So it is not a question of referentiality, there is no language that is not referential in a certain way. And as you very well know, when I said there is 'nothing outside of the text' I didn't mean 'text' in the sense of what is written in a book; I *first* generalized the concept of text, of trace – 'text' is not just, say, literature or philosophy but life in general. Life after theory is a text. Life is a text, but then we have to change the rules, change the concept of text and that is what I try to do.

There are, of course, types of narrative by historians which I never try to reduce to literature – that would be silly, and people who are under the illusion that things *are* that silly confuse literature and what is *not* literature. But, if you don't take into account, or pay attention to the possibility of a serious historical narrative signed by a historian being a lie, a fiction or a perjury, then you miss the reference. You miss the real things. The real may be a lie. If historians were simply relying upon historical sources we could not say their work was in any way critical, but when a historian or a historiographer does pay attention to fiction – let's take the case of Hayden White, for instance – immediately people get angry and, not trying to understand, charge him with saying that 'everything goes, history is fiction'. Look at Carlo Ginsburg who got mad because a historian was simply paying attention to the fact that, in historical discourse, serious historical discourse, there was rhetoric, there were tropes and sometimes fictions.

Now, the case of Paul de Man. Let me be clear; first of all, de Man was my friend, he is still my friend. He is dead, and I try to show in *The Politics of Friendship* that it's through death, or after death, that friendship, the test of friendship, is demanded. One must decide whether or not to remain faithful after the death of someone who's not here to check, verify or respond; the other one is just not here to know. And that, for me, is the condition of fidelity, the absolute condition of fidelity.

So, Paul de Man is still my friend. We shared a lot of things in theory; *but, but* ... I disagree with him on a number of points. I didn't say so immediately during the de Man affair because, strategically, if I had said at that moment in 1987, 'Well, you know, Paul de Man, the way he handles deconstruction is not exactly my way,' that would have been terrible, terrible. People would have exploited this. So I didn't say that, but I knew, and he knew too, there were differences between us and now slowly, slowly, I'm trying to say this. And there is a long text which was published last year and which I republished in French – now it's being republished in English entitled *Typewriter Ribbon* – in which I raise this question of confession in Rousseau, and there are a number of points at which I try, while being as friendly as possible, to locate the possible disagreement. That is what I did this morning too. In a certain way, I betrayed him, but out of fidelity.

The case this morning, the specificity of this promise, had to do with the fact that we, I, had to read a fiction, a literary fiction, which has the status of a fiction according to a number of laws, of rules, belonging to the history of literature, which is the history of the Law, or the Right in Europe. We know that, in principle, according to the law, the author is not the narrator, that the book, being a fiction, has nothing to do in principle with reality and so on and so forth. But this fictionality is protected by a number of historical rules; sometimes it's very difficult, especially now, to understand and respect these rules, because there are texts today which belong to literature *and* to something else, and it is difficult to draw the border. We *know* that there is no such thing as what they called twenty or forty years ago 'literariness,' that is, an essence of the literary, as if language *could* be literary in itself, intrinsically – there is no such thing. The same sentence, the same page, may belong to literature in a given context and to everyday life or newspapers in a different context; so, no, there is no intrinsic analysis which can tell us that *this* text is literary and *this* text is not. It is merely a set of conventions, the contextual evaluation, which tells us that this text *here* functions as literary and *there* functions as everyday, as, say, newspaper or legal text. It is a matter of functioning not essence. So in the case of this text this morning we know that the book, that you have seen, functions as a literary product. *But*, because I told you that de Man told me that he was the real referent of this fiction, which remains a fiction, you have to trust me, of course. I could have lied. It could be another fiction. Imagine that I had some interest in telling you this – de Man is dead, he won't come and protest. Imagine that I simply said to myself, 'Well, I will go to Loughborough and tell them that de Man told me so and so.' No one can check this. But I referred to something I call '*real*, real life': 'In real life de Man told me, etc., etc . . . '. I did this for a number of reasons, a number of different reasons – one being what I thought I had to say about my *own* life, my personal history and my own history in the academy and my own relationship to de Man. I thought I had to make this public, first. Then, I wanted to draw your attention, and the attention of others, to this very difficult question of responsibility in literature and outside literature. I wanted also to follow the questions of perjury, marriage, forgiveness and the transaction between all these necessities in life and in theory. Life is not a literary phenomenon, not totally literary.

I should here bring in Christianity, since you could consider this morning's lecture to be a lecture on Christianity – I know that some of you here are interested in this. At the end of the lecture someone who is Muslim asked me about marriage in Islam. Well, as far as I know, monogamy is not the rule, the *absolute* rule, in Islam, nor in Judaism; monogamy was imposed in Judaism very late in Europe – in Algeria, where I come from, two or three generations ago monogamy was not an imperative. So I told this person that, to my knowledge, the sacred, sacramental oath in modern marriage is a Christian phenomenon. It is neither Jewish nor Islamic. The question, then, was whether there would be no perjury in a culture in which monogamy is not the rule? To get married twice without being divorced is a form of perjury in America or Europe; but this legal principle is Christian *in spirit*. So, perhaps, the lecture was simply on Christianity, the United States and the academy, or was a transaction with all these interests.

Would this have anything to do with 'an ethics of reading'? I don't know. I know that it's a title of a book by another friend of mine, Hillis Miller. What I said in response to Nick earlier, about being true to a text by being untrue to it, is a strange sort of ethics of reading. But what is ethics in the case when you have to negotiate between two contradictory injunctions? I never call this an 'ethics of reading', myself, but if I had to justify this phrase I would say this: of course, there are competing, conflicting injunctions – to be true to the grammar of the text *and* at the same time to do something else, to distort, but to distort in a good way, to do something else. There are ethics precisely because there is this contradiction, because there *is* no rule. There are ethics because I have to *invent* the rule; and there would be no responsibility if I knew the rule, if I knew how to read, if the injunction were simple: 'Well, you have to read simply – there is a norm, there is a rule and you have to do your duty.' If there was such a norm there would be no responsibility. There is responsibility only because there are these aporetic structures in which I have to respond to two injunctions, different and incompatible. That's where responsibility starts, when I *don't* know what to do. If I knew what to do, well, I would apply the rule, and teach my students to apply the rule. But would that be ethical? I'm not sure. I would consider this unethical. Ethics start when you don't know what to do, when there is this gap between knowledge and action, and you have to take responsibility for inventing the new rule which doesn't exist. You invent the rule when you read the text in a way which produces another rule responding to the text, or countersigning the text. This is very dangerous and you have no guarantee. An ethics with guarantees is not an ethics. If you have an ethics with some insurance, and you know that if you are wrong the insurance will pay, it isn't ethics. Ethics is dangerous.

Nicholas Royle: The extraordinary consistency of your work is, I suppose, partly what we've been hearing or what we've been invited to think about so far today. I wonder if I could ask a question about something which seems to me to be extraordinarily consistent as a kind of absence, perhaps. It's a question about the uncanny. Your lecture this morning struck me as in various ways uncanny, not least in its exposure of Stéphane's need to encrypt while unveiling the secret; this relates to what you say, in various different texts, about that which is *foreign* to the opposition of veiling and unveiling (in 'A Silkworm of One's Own', for instance) or 'alien to the very figure of the veil' (in *Monolingualism of the Other*).

In these respects it seems to me that you are concerned with a sense of the uncanny that elaborates, while differing from, what Freud says, quoting Schelling, in his essay 'Das Unheimliche': 'The uncanny is what should have remained secret and hidden but has come to light.' At least since a couple of footnotes in 'The Double Session' in 1970, you have said, on the subject of your reading of Freud's essay on the uncanny, that it is 'to be continued'. I think it's possible to argue that everything you've written since 1970 can be read as a continuing engagement with the question of the uncanny. Sometimes it seems to me that your engagement with the uncanny is more oblique or implicit, and, at other times – for example, in 'Le Facteur de la Vérité', or *Spectres of Marx* – it's more explicit. So, I'd like to ask how you see your relation to Freud's essay in terms of what you've been writing over the past 30 years. I wonder if we can still hope for the essay or book on this topic as it seemed to be promised in those footnotes of 30 years ago. And finally, I wonder if you'd be willing to say something about the uncanny today, possibly following on from the remarks that you were just making about Christianity – that's to say, how we might construe the relation between the uncanny and religion.

Jacques Derrida: Thank you. In a certain way, you're right – everything I have written since the footnote on the uncanny that you mentioned could be inscribed under this title; this could be done. I could, if I had time, show that everything refers to this uncanniness. And in a certain way the only thing which interests me is the uncanny, which, as you know, is a translation, in this context, of *das Unheimliche* which in German means two opposite things, things which are in conflict: 'the strangest' *and* 'the most familiar'. Freud starts with this apparent antinomy in the single word. But in the foot-note that you mention I tried to show how Freud puts aside the question of literature; although all his exam-ples come from literature, when he addresses the ques-tion of literature he avoids it in a certain way. So I tried to do exactly the opposite. You are right, therefore – in an oblique way, everything I have written has to do with the uncanny, especially in relation to the question of spectrality, or ghosts. There are ghosts everywhere in my texts – everywhere; not only in *Spectres of Marx* but long before, there are ghosts everywhere. So, this morning, what was uncanny? Well, there were a very great number of things which looked uncanny within the novel, but also on the border between the novel and so-called real life. There is the secret, the manifest secret, the secret and the light within the novel: Stéphane Chalier is encrypting a secret and the narrator doesn't know finally what happened. He is his close friend, his only friend, but he doesn't know what happened. So there is a secret and nevertheless the secret is absolutely manifest, in full light, in full daylight; so there is this ambiguity between the secret and the non-secret. The narrator identifies with Stéphane, the main character – nevertheless, he remains absolutely other, absolutely different. And I might say the same about Paul de Man; he remained a secret to me. People think that since he was a close friend we knew one another, that I knew what his life was. I knew nothing and still today he remains absolutely enigmatic to me. Sometimes in his texts, and above all in his life, I *don't* know him. I know almost nothing about him.

Now, in, let's say, theory and philosophy, the way I try to pay attention publicly, or not publicly, to *das Unheimliche* is not simply by reading Freud but by reading the word in German and especially in Heidegger. In Heidegger *das Unheimliche* is very present, and in places where the stakes are very high. I can't do this now, but in some of my seminars I try to locate the most important places when Heidegger uses the word *unheimlich*, and it's always the most decisive moments. So I try to understand what *das Unheimliche* means in this German epoch, the first part of the twentieth century – why is it the best name, the best concept, for something which resists consistency, system, semantic identity? Why is it *the* experience, the most thinking experience in Freud *and* in Heidegger?

Now for the last part of your remarks – the questions about Christianity and marriage. You know, one could say, *after* Kierkegaard, that if Christianity prescribes marriage it's mad; *das Unheimliche* is, of course, mad, the uncanny is a form of madness. This doesn't mean that one is against Christianity or marriage, but we're invited to reconsider what madness is. Perhaps we start thinking, start promising, start being responsible, *by being mad*; taking responsibility or making a decision is madness because you do so only when there are two competing, conflicting injunctions and that is the definition of madness. You know the theory of the double bind – well, a double bind generates madness, for when you are confronted with two incompatible injunctions you start being mad. When you want to make someone mad, you put him or her under a double bind, insisting on it, not just for a minute but *constantly*. If the double bind is the condition for responsibility, or ethics, then ethics are mad. Kierkegaard was certainly very close to thinking that to take on a responsibility implies some madness, and getting married is such a responsibility. To promise fidelity for a whole life to someone who finally you don't know, who finally will change, is madness. And if you distinguish between thinking and reason – that is, knowledge – then thinking has to do with some sort of madness. So perhaps I could imagine a Christian who says, 'Well, what Jesus Christ did was mad; he was precisely opposing his own madness, his own hubris, to what was considered reason at the time.' This may be interpreted in *favour* of Christianity. Christianity is the only mad religion; which is perhaps, the explanation for its survival – it deconstructs itself and *survives* by deconstructing itself. So, this morning, I didn't conclude anything. I wanted just to put these words together – Christianity, marriage, madness – and then everyone takes his or her responsibility.

Faith, of course, is madness. If you want to experience faith as something reassuring and wise, something reliable or probable, it's not faith. Faith must be mad, or absurd, as they say sometimes. That's the condition of faith – the distinction between faith and knowledge, for instance.

Sarah Wood: After these remarks, I feel a sense of anti-climax when I hear my own voice. I also felt at moments in your paper a sense of bathos, 'a sinking in a narrative' – a kind of high moment, a good moment followed by an anticlimax, a falling away. I'm not saying this is something bad but it's something I felt. For example, in the transition towards the end of your paper, you're quoting from the final scene of *Le parjure* and we're on the island, it's night, or rather twilight; we're in the company of an impassive woman and there is a disappearance, a dis-appearance with which we identify. It's a moving moment of dramatic emotion and then – this isn't the only example but it's the most striking – we're returned to a particular moment, there is a postscript to your paper, we return, we're among the professors again. I wondered if you'd say something about bathos in your work.

Jacques Derrida: I'm very grateful for this question because, although I've no rigorous answer to it, it points to something which matters a lot to me when I write – that is, the composition, or rhythm. And this rhythm matters more than *what* I say, so to speak, more than the content. But, in fact, my answer, on the example that you've chosen, would be more trivial, because at some point the lecture was too long and I felt – even when I wrote it – that I should break, interrupt and change the tone, leave something suspended. It's a question of economy that I always face when I write; I know that my lecture will be too long, the article will be too long, and I have to calculate the changes in tone so as to break at the best moment. But I cannot justify this. If I had been asked to write a 200-page volume then I would have spent more time with the last scene, which deserves it; I could add a lot of things, and everything, the whole 'landscape', would have changed and so too the rhythm. So there is something aleatory in this. I do, though, try (according to what I call again and again the transaction of negotiation) to combine the aleatory character of the context – 'I had to stop here' – with the internal necessity of the composition.

But it is true that the attention I pay to the composition has to do not simply with my own taste but also with what was at stake on this occasion, in this text. I wanted my lecture to look, to some extent, like a sort of novel or artefact, another composition, as if I didn't need a text any more, didn't need Thomas and de Man any more. Yes and no. I don't know if it's a theoretical discourse or a fiction, and you'll never know because you have to trust me. You have to trust me when I say, 'I bear witness that de Man said this and de Man was my friend.' It's not scientific, you have to trust me. So the question of the oath and the possible fiction, or lie is not only incorporated but embodied *en abîme* within my text. Someone could come and say, 'Well, what is essential in this lecture is the fact that you came, that you said "de Man told me", and that this was perhaps a fiction.' This is the main point – that you have to trust me without any possibility of checking. Just trust me, that's the main event.

Christopher Norris: You were obviously fascinated and intrigued by that particular line in the novel, 'Just imagine, I wasn't thinking', or 'I wasn't thinking about it.' And I would guess that your fascination goes back again to that quite early essay of yours on J. L. Austin where you raise this whole question about Austin's idea of 'sincerity conditions' and point out that it's problematic to specify criteria for what should count properly as a sincere or authentic speech-act. You remark that very often it doesn't matter whether someone presently or actually means what they say. So, for instance, if a minister of religion conducting a marriage service were to say, after having conducted the service according to the usual rituals and conventions, 'Sorry, that was just a practice run', or 'Sorry, I was joking', or 'I was drunk', or 'My mind wasn't on it', or 'Just imagine, I wasn't thinking about it', it wouldn't matter so long as the correct words had been spoken by all parties concerned and so long as the circumstances were appropriate. I was thinking, in connection with this, that your own work raises questions – sometimes quite difficult questions for earnest-minded exegetes like me – as to whether we should take you (so to speak) 'at your word', as 'really meaning' what you say, or perhaps as rehearsing certain speech-acts to which you are not committed in a straightforward, 'authentic' way. I'm thinking of an essay like 'Of an Apocalyptic Tone Recently Adopted in Philosophy', which is a very elusive essay, one where it's very hard to know when you're speaking, as it were, in your own voice, *in propria persona*, and when we're hearing a kind of oblique paraphrase, a free-indirect rendition of Kant's views, or Hamann's views, or Jacobi's views, or the views of other contending parties in the great debate around the topic 'What is Enlightenment?'

This raises the whole question of – in the title of a book by Stanley Cavell – *Must We Mean What We Say?* And, how are we to know when *other people* mean what they say? or indeed, what they mean – what their speech-acts signify – when they *do* 'sincerely' mean what they say, but cannot know or foresee what future effects their words might have, or under what changed circumstances they might be held to their word? This issue is obviously crucial in the case of Paul de Man. And of course it raises difficult questions in the context of law, especially of contract law, where so much depends on the idea, or legal fiction, that persons (or subjects before the law) *can and should* be held responsible for past actions, speech-acts, verbal undertakings and so forth. A whole range of legal presuppositions – indeed the whole edifice of law – would simply collapse if we didn't have some sort of working notion of what it means to be committed to what one is saying, both to mean it when one says it and later feel bound to honour that performative commitment. This morning you raised this question of the two senses of 'perjury': on the one hand, breaking one's word later on, simply changing one's mind; and on the other hand, the more problematical case of someone who doesn't mean what they say *at the very moment when they say it* and who enters private mental reservations or ironic disclaimers. So I wonder if you could address this general question of meaning what we say and the problems that arise with Austin's treatment of the issue.

Jacques Derrida: Thank you. First of all, when I paid attention to the phrase, *figurez-vous que je n'y pensais pas* ('Imagine that I was not thinking about it') I was thinking that there is a question of figure. In French, in everyday language, *je n'y pensais pas* means 'I wasn't paying attention'. It has not the seriousness or the gravity of Heidegger's *Was heisst Denken? (What Is Called Thinking?)*. That's why I entitled the first part of my lecture, 'What is called not thinking?' What do we do when we don't think? Simply, we don't seriously pay attention. It's a question of degree, it's not a question of thinking. So, do we mean what we say? Instead of addressing this issue, this canonical problem that you mention, I would go back to the question of lying and I would argue that it is always impossible to have proof regarding a lie. You cannot demonstrate that someone was meaning what he said or was not meaning what he said. It's impossible. You may have some probabilities, you may guess, you may infer, or reconstruct the possibility but you cannot provide a proof of any lie because the supposed liar can always tell you, 'Well, I didn't mean it. I meant something else, and you're not in my head.' And that's what Husserl, in his *Cartesian Meditations*, demonstrated – that we have no access in the form of an originary intuition to what's going on on the side of the other ego. We have analogies, or reconstructions but we have no direct access to what the other is thinking. The other can always tell you, 'Well, I said this but I didn't mean it, so perhaps I was wrong, I didn't lie,' so you cannot prove that someone is lying or has been perjuring. 'I didn't think of it ... I didn't mean it.'

Let's go back to the example of the marriage:

> I said 'I do' but I didn't mean it. In fact I did not realize what was going on and, of course, that was a mistake; I misunderstood the situation, I was misusing words, I'm not very good at English, I don't know what 'I do' means exactly, I'm from continental Europe . . .

Because, in legal space, the assumption is that the legal subject has a full understanding of grammar and the lexicon, he is supposed to understand the law and the language of the law. If someone doesn't understand fully then he may argue that he didn't mean what he said, he used this word without meaning it. And in addition to this a number of consequences might follow. A lie is something that you can never prove. You can never prove that someone made a false testimony. It's impossible. You can prove that someone said something wrong, something false but not necessarily deliberately. The intention and the 'deliberately' is beyond any theoretical, scientific demonstration. There are a number of consequences to this.

Now, beyond this problem of not meaning what one says or not meaning intentionally, there is the problem of the voices that you raised and the question of psychoanalysis. There are many voices in me. I've not only one voice, and sometimes another voice speaks through me: my unconscious, a symptom; there are a number of inhabitants in me. We know, even if we're not convinced by psychoanalysis, that we speak through a number of voices – a masculine voice, a feminine voice. That's why I let many voices speak in my texts. Sometimes I say, 'Well, I can't write a text with one voice,' and so I write the text with a number of voices – different tones, different positions, different demands. So I can say, 'Well, the one who said "I do" is someone in me but there is another one and another one and another one and I'm more than one.' And what can you object to this? But the legal system implies that the legal subject is just one, just one, and that when he says 'yes', it's 'yes', there is no other one saying 'no', and that this one is speaking fully a single language, that he understands the language, understands the English law and understands the questions of the attorney, and the court and the policeman. And we know it's not simply a theoretical assumption. We know, especially now, that there are a number of people who live in our countries – England and France, for instance – who don't understand fully the language and they are in a situation where they cannot simply behave responsibly before the law and it's a major political, legal problem. So, in the organization of nation states such as ours and the United States, the assumption, the main assumption, is that there is one major language, the language of the law – English, for instance, in the United States and here – and that every legal subject is supposed to understand the language fully and in a transparent way and there is no place, no room left, for rhetoric, or for twilights, and no place for the unconscious. The legal system today in Western countries – all over the world but especially in Western countries – does not recognize something like psychoanalysis, does not recognize that there are symptoms for which we're not responsible. When there is a crime it is not necessarily a free and deliberately committed murder. So, there is a huge gap here between the political and legal system and what we know is a fact, a necessity – the multiplicity of languages and multiplicity of voices.

To go back, just for one more second, to the question of meaning: do we mean what we say? For someone to mean what he or she says fully there must be the possibility for *not* meaning, for lying or for meaning something else, or if not lying then simply meaning something else – not in order to deceive the other but simply because the language is such that we say something else. We always say something other than what we say. So, for someone to mean what he or she says, the possibility must remain always open for *not* meaning, for meaning something else. If you close this possibility then there is no language anymore, there is no language. So, to have the possibility of the authentic, sincere and full meaning of what one says, the possibility of the failure, or of the lie, or of something else, must remain open. That's the structure of language. There would be no truth otherwise. I insist on this because if I didn't say this I would be considered someone who is opposed to truth or simply doesn't believe in truth. No, I am attached to truth, but I simply recall that for the truth to be true and for the meaning to be meaningful the possibility of a misunderstanding or lie or something else must remain, structurally, always open. That's the condition for truth to be the truth and for sincerity to be sincere.

QUESTIONS FROM THE FLOOR

Leila Prelec: I heard your lecture entirely as a lecture about Christianity and, when you were talking, I couldn't help thinking about Jesus' interruption of Judaism and that interruption's production of a new rule, as you would say. And this made me wonder: to what extent are you talking in this lecture about yourself as a Jew after the Christian event? Because you are so responsible, and so preoccupied with responsibility, do you feel you must respond in some way to the Christian event? Would you say that you are trying to make, personally, some sense of Jesus' 'heresy' as a Jew? Indeed, would you say that the acolytes who followed him in some sense betrayed him and those that didn't follow him, like yourself, are in a sense more true to him?

Jacques Derrida: You should write something, another novel in this direction, it would be very interesting. Of course, my lecture, as I said a moment ago, *was* in fact about Christianity in some sense, but I must confess I didn't think of Jesus himself in this, and his experience. I could have done – you, you have done so. As for my own involvement as a Jew: this is so difficult, my being Jewish, this is a very difficult issue. I'm not sure I'm Jewish, I'm not sure. Of course, I was born Jewish, I'm not denying this and I am now to be true to this. Nevertheless, it's not simple, as you can easily imagine. And so, I am and I am not Jewish, and I am and I am not Christian, because I live in a Christian culture, no doubt. I've been raised in a Christian culture, so even if I'm not Christian in the full sense of the word, I'm not un-Christian. No doubt, I'm constantly struggling in this space that you define, but what disturbed me in your question is that you define responsibility as something Christian or something to be experienced in relation to Christianity as if there is no Jewish responsibility, I mean no responsibility in Jewish ethics which is, of course, wrong.

Leila Prelec: No, I mean that as a Jew you might be responsible to Christianity.

Jacques Derrida: Of course I can't answer briefly your question. It's true that everything I do, everything I do, is haunted by this question of Judaism, Christianity ... and Islam, *and Islam*. I try again and again not to forget Islam in these texts – 'Faith and Knowledge', for instance.[3] And if I may, if I may refer to this: there will be a book of 'mine', so to speak, because it's made up of various texts of mine with an introduction by a young friend named Gil Anidjar who, in his introduction, insists upon precisely the couple Judaism/Islam no less than the couple Judaism/Christianity. So, it's very complicated. The simplest answer would be, 'Yes', I'm constantly trying to discover – this is not original – I am constantly trying to understand, or stabilize what happened between Judaism and Christianity and Islam, and I can't say much more now. But you're right it's everywhere in my texts. It's not simply a responsibility for someone – for example, a Jew toward Christianity – if we attempt to think what responsibility is, what it means to be responsible. And it means different things whether you are Jewish, Christian or Muslim; there *are* responsibilities in all three, and there are other examples, but in these three so-called 'monotheistic' religions the concept of responsibility certainly occurs. I can't get into this now but I try – in *The Gift of Death*, for instance – to address the question of responsibility: between philosophy and religion, philosophy and Christianity, Christianity and Islam. So, if I may, I will postpone my answer and refer you to, at least these two texts, *The Gift of Death* and 'Faith and Knowledge', and perhaps this text to come called *Acts of Religion*. I wrote *Acts of Religion* but don't read me, read the introduction by Gil Anidjar.[4]

Michael Newman: I have a question about forgetting and the status of forgetting in relation to what you have to say. It seems to me that the aporias that arise, arise from taking notions like promise and responsibility to a kind of hyperbolic degree. If it wasn't a hyperbolic responsibility, if it was only a bit of responsibility, you wouldn't have the problem of the irresponsibility necessarily involved in responsibility. You could just be responsible some of the time. You said in the lecture that you can't reasonably expect a finite subject to remember presently all their responsibilities, and you also mentioned that God doesn't have to remember or doesn't have to promise. That made me think of Nietzsche in *The Genealogy of Morals* when he says that a memory has to be created through pain in order to make a being that could keep promises. And Nietzsche advocates or associates life with active forgetfulness or active forgetting which is, of course, paradoxical – since, how can one actively forget, you'd have to forget to forget, in which case you'd be, in a sense, passively forgetting. Nevertheless, in Heidegger as well there is an almost positive assertion of forgetting with the *lethe* in *aletheia* (the forgetting in truth-as-unforgetting). So, the question that I wanted to ask in relation to what you're saying about promising and responsibility is: what is the relation between the quasi-infinite status of the demand and the finitude implied by forgetting? Sometimes it sounds like forgetting is a kind of defect but it obviously isn't because it's the very core of responsibility. So, how can these two aspects relate to each other?

Jacques Derrida: This is why, although I didn't say this in the lecture perhaps, this is why the question of forgetting is not simply psychological, is not simply a faculty. It's something which happens beyond any psychology. That's at the centre of what Heidegger refers to as 'Being', Being with a capital 'B'. And, of course, when you say a finite being cannot remember every thing or every duty you immediately make a leap from, let's say, the psychological, or anthropological level to some ontological structure. Forgetting is not simply a psychological fact. Now, although I think, at least I obviously think, that no finite being can remember every thing and every injunction, so cannot be infinitely responsible, I also think that, nevertheless, that's another contradiction, that responsibility must be infinite. That's why I always feel not responsible enough, because I'm finite and because there are an infinite number of others to whom or for whom or from whom I should be responsible. I'm always not responsible enough, and responsibility is infinite or it *is* not; but I cannot be responsible *to some extent* in the strict sense of 'responsibility'. There *is* a field in which responsibility might be, can be, limited, such as trade, or commerce; but, in ethics the responsibility to the other is infinite *or* it is not. That's why I always feel guilty. Not because I cultivate bad conscience – I don't like bad conscience – but because of the structure of responsibility, its infinity, although I am a finite being. That is why I'm always unequal to my responsibility, always disproportionate to my own finitude and the field of responsibility that I have – infinite responsibility towards the other, towards God, and so on and so forth.

Nietzsche speaks, and I often refer to this, of *aktiven Vergesslichkeit*,[5] a deliberate attempt to forget – we don't forget by accident. For Nietzsche, we do our best to forget – that is, *not* to accept the burden of responsibility in the manner of a Christian, for that is to be like the donkey, to be just crushed by the necessity to say 'Yes' to memory and obligation.[6] We should repeat not the *Ja Ja,* or 'Yes Yes', of the donkey but the *Ja Ja* of the one who comes to repeat the affirmation, *Ja Ja*. And in order to be true to becoming, to repeat the affirmation in a gay, joyful manner, you have to stop remembering, to stop taking on your shoulders the burden of responsibility, of memory. Life is forgetting. You wouldn't survive without forgetting. So, you have to actively forget. In that case it is paradoxical, as you say; you cannot decide to forget. What Nietzsche meant by *aktiven Vergesslichkeit* is not that you have to remember what you have to forget. It is simply that you go on living and affirming and saying *Ja Ja*. To come back to what I said about the marriage a moment ago and the 'I do', or the 'Yes' – in French we say 'Yes': when I say 'Yes', when I promise to be true to someone in a marriage, I not only promise, not only say 'Yes' now but I've already promised to say 'Yes' in a minute, in an hour, tomorrow and for eternity. Now, in order to repeat the 'Yes', which is included in the structure of the affirmation, the 'I do', I must both keep the memory and also forget. For me to say 'I do' today, the same 'I do' as yesterday or as 50 years ago, I must remember and I must also forget, otherwise it wouldn't be a new 'I do'. For it to be new, for it to be an event, an innovation, some forgetfulness must be at work, *at work*. I must forget in order to perform, or to experience a new event. That's the condition for not forgetting. If you just remember then nothing happens. So that, I think, is what Nietzsche had in mind, that in order to repeat the affirmation you have to forget, and that's what life is – forgetting. This way of forgetting is not futile, or simply a destruction, it's the ethical way of being ready for the event, for what is coming. And this can be thought in Christian terms even though it was anti-Christian, of course, on the part of Nietzsche. But you can, for instance, turn the *Ja Ja* into a Christian or Jewish Messianicity – a readiness for the event, for the one who comes. Others forget, but you can be just ready for the future, for when he comes. And so forgetting is not a bad thing; it's a condition of fidelity to forget.

Michael Newman: Can I just ask if there is a conflict within infinite responsibility?

Jacques Derrida: Yes, of course there is conflict, there is an ongoing conflict.

2

value after theory

Frank Kermode

Michael Payne: Ten years ago I had the fortunate occasion to review many of the books and articles published by Frank Kermode during the previous forty years. At that time, four distinctive features seemed to me to mark the variety of his career as a critic. One was his sustained attention to literature both as a body of texts, and to the literary as a value. Second, his commitment, through the production of journalistic and scholarly reviews, to fostering an appreciation of literary value in what he called the wider literary public. Third, his persistent critical investigation of the politics of canonicity, and of interpretative institutions, from ancient times to modern. And then fourth, his cautious investments in literary theory. That theoretical caution is perhaps best expressed in the prologue to his book, *An Appetite for Poetry*, published in 1989; there he writes 'my sense of the matter is simply that it would be quite wrong to deplore theory as such, but quite right to contest some of its claims; there has not been a time within living memory when it did not appear to some that theory was swamping literature'. In addition to his own writing, Frank Kermode made at least two other major contributions to what now may seem to have been theory's conquest, or appropriation of literary criticism: one, of course, was his editing of the Modern Masters series, which includes Chris Norris's book on Derrida, Malcolm Bowie's on Lacan, Jonathan Culler's on Barthes; the other was Frank's offering of a seminar on literary theory at University College, London when he was the benign dictator of the English Department there beginning in the late 1960s, and that seminar ended in 1974. I think that was when Frank left University College for Cambridge.

In the prologue to *The Art of Telling* (1983), Frank confesses that 'no other phase of my academic life has given me so much pleasure and instruction as that seminar on literary theory'. Its members included Jonathan Culler, Jacqueline Rose, Annette Lavers and Christopher Norris; Roland Barthes himself also made a rare appearance. As Frank himself says about that seminar,

> not the least of the qualifications of these and many other friends was a willingness to express lively disagreement without rancour; another was to examine one's own prejudices as well as other's, and to preserve a tone of good humour in the midst of the most serious, even the most fierce exchanges. I think we all know that there have been many discussions of literary theory not marked by such civility.

The major tension in Frank's work, especially during the past ten years, or so it seems to me, has been between his constant commitment to literary value and his omnivorous intellectual appetite, which includes an apparently irrepressible interest in theory, even though he keeps telling us that he doesn't in the least find that that matches his appetite for poetry. The recent publication of his book, *Shakespeare's Language*, offers the opportunity to reflect on the theoretical dimensions of his major critical work. If I may be forgiven for putting such a complex subject so simply, I would say that theory is about how we self-reflectively see things, and that theories, therefore, are more or less transparent, opaque or translucent. If opaque, theories, by calling attention only to the way things are being seen, rather than also to the things themselves, constitute one extreme. Transparent theories, by insisting with Wittgenstein, for example, in *Philosophical Investigations*, that he has no theories at all, constitute another extreme. Translucent theories, like lightly frosted, tinted or misty windows, never let us forget that we are looking from somewhere to somewhere else, and that there is something between us and what we gaze upon, or what gazes upon us. Critical theory begins with such an awareness as this, in the interest of being critically reflective, and it seems to me that critical theory was already fully at work in Frank's earliest books. For example, he writes in his introduction to *English Pastoral Poetry*, published in 1952, that 'the first condition of pastoral is that it is an urban product' – here we already seem to be launched into theory; that is, we are already being cautioned to be aware of an ironic distance that is always there wherever a sophisticated, critical, urban intelligence – Marvell's, for instance – gazes upon even the most natural and simple of lives. This suggests that civility, irony and theory, belong together. We meet this trio again in Frank

Kermode's magisterial introduction to the Arden edition of *The Tempest*, first published in 1954, where he writes 'art is not only a beneficent magic, in contrast to an evil one, it is the ordination of civility with control of appetite, the transformation of nature by breathing and learning; it is even the means of Grace'. Although those sentences were written half a century ago, the values they proclaim have remained constant in Frank Kermode's later work. There is a great deal in his book *Shakespeare's Language* that suggests that poetry and theory have more in common than we often admit; for example, Frank offers a particularly fine commentary on Bushy's speech of consolation to the Queen in *Richard II*, 'Each substance of a grief hath twenty shadows,/Which shows like grief itself but is not so,/For sorrow's eyes glazed with blinding tears,/Divides one thing entire into many objects,/Like perspectives, which, rightly gazed upon,/Show nothing but confusion.' The two key points in his commentary are that this language conveys a sense of the active immediacy of Bushy's thinking, as though the thought is totally in the struggle of the language: we are witnesses to it at the very moment when it is being thought and spoken. The other point concerns perspective as an interestingly muddled allusion to anamorphic pictures, such as Holbein's *The Ambassadors*; whether the Queen's perspective is like a prism or not, as she gazes through her tears, is not perhaps as important as Bushy's thinking how she might be seeing things now. As modernist readers, Frank Kermode's commentary argues, we have come to appreciate Bushy's muddle in ways that Dr Johnson did not. Hovering over this discussion is a phrase from Sonnet 24, 'Perspective, it is best painter's art'; if critical theory is a means of keeping us aware of how we see things, so too is Shakespeare's language, especially, or so Frank argues, after 1600. Rather than argue that such a reading as this is possible, for example, because of deconstructive theory, it might be more accurate to say that it is Shakespeare's creation of Bushy in the act of empathic theory, or theory-making, that illuminates deconstructive reading. That would enable us to understand better Derrida's insistence, as for example, in his Amnesty lectures, that deconstruction is a 'Yes' – an affirmation of the multiplicity of meaning. Theory, therefore, is but one source of the protocols of reading; another has always been the self-reflectiveness of literary language.

The volume devoted to Frank Kermode in our Bucknell Lectures in Literary Theory series[1] includes a bibliography, compiled by Keith Walker, of Frank's books and major scholarly articles published between 1947 and 1988: there are more than three hundred items in that list, and of course now the bibliography is well out of date. I mention these facts not to embarrass Frank, but rather to emphasize the necessary incompleteness of my very brief sketch of the range and variety of his writing and the depth of his project.

Frank Kermode: Well thank you very much, Mike, you're much clearer about my position than I am. What is obvious from what you say, is that I've been doing this kind of thing for a long time; it's arguable that I've been doing it for too long. One of the consequences of that is to have lived through a constantly changing relationship with the institutions which shelter speculation, whether it's literary or theoretical. As for that seminar which you mentioned around about 1968 to 1970-odd, in London, one of the joys of it, I see now, was that we were a minority, we were people who were doing something new and anti-institutional; that the very Department in which we were holding these seminars was not interested in what we were doing. We thought 'this is the future'; the people who provided the fire for those discussions – Stephen Heath, Jonathan Culler, Chris Norris, Jacqueline Rose (who was my student) – were all younger than I and they were less struck, perhaps, than I was by the way in which we were swimming against the tide. Later, of course, the theoretical approach (we call it that very vaguely) to the study of literature was institutionalized; so in fact, in order to stay outside institutionalization, you have to take a position, a rather uneasy one like my present one, which is to *oppose*. I find that, having belonged to institutions of this kind myself, for many years, I've always disliked them and, when I left them in 1982, when I cheerfully resigned from Cambridge, I was back where I wanted to be; that is to say, outside. Consequently, I've always looked at what was once so exciting, in very primitive forms, perhaps, in 1968 or 1970, as now – in its present efflorescence – something that I ought to resist. I think that, as Mike Payne has just said, we now have a mode of talking about art in general; since the aesthetic is out of fashion, we have a mode of talking about it which is self-reflexive. We took a perfectly legitimate step to say 'let's think about what thinking about literature means', but that step could be an endless series, because you could then go on to think about what thinking about literature means, and so on. So you rise to what some have called the meta-level, and meanwhile the prime object, or the excuse for it all to happen, recedes into the distance, and becomes, in some ways, rather despised: by that I mean Literature.

Literature – it is sometimes said, triumphantly – is an invention only about two hundred years ago, and this is regarded as a kind of telling blow against Literature. Well, lots of things were invented in the last two hundred years that we rather approve of, and if we did invent literature two hundred years ago, well, very good, I think it an excellent idea: one of the brighter notions of the eighteenth century. So it shouldn't be totally distanced by people thinking about how you think about it, and so on, and so on. In the booklet for this conference, John Schad has singled out a remark of mine about opening a door in the late 1960s which 'let in many unexpected guests';[2] I don't remember writing that sentence, but in fact it seems to me to be very true, because what happened was that the whole scope of the theoretical approach widened in the most extraordinary way after those early years. So theory became not theory of literature, it became Theory, it involved everything, it involved philosophy, politics and so on, and so you lose the sense in which you could satisfy the desire that a lot of people had, and perhaps fewer people now have, to come into intimate contact with literary texts.

I suppose I should continue the little tale of my relationship with institutionalized literary scholarship by
observing that it's so long since I had any direct contact
with an institution and I'm so old, in fact, that I don't
really care. There's also the fact that it's possible for me
now to allow the view of theory spreading out in this
imperialist way over all forms of thought, to view that
with perfect calm. This is because, for one thing, I'm
fairly sure that it can't actually continue indefinitely –
nothing does in this field. If you think about it, there are
certain kinds of literary theory which have kept the
attention of people interested for a very long time; you
think of Aristotle, for example, people still argue about
what is meant by the *Poetics* and it still seems relevant
to a great deal in thinking. But if you don't go back as
far as that; if you go back to the time when the study of
literature was institutionalized, say a hundred years ago,
maybe even two hundred years ago, in some older
American universities and in some British universities
too, you find that the history of the subject very often
can be represented as the history of certain people,
usually men, who make themselves immense reputations
and get a considerable following, and then go out like
lights. If you think back, even as far back as the late
1950s, the name of Northrop Frye, for example, was
absolutely omnipotent in those years – *now*, as far as I'm
aware, very few people pay much attention to Frye. Of
course, he's been dead a decade, or so, but for a while
he ruled the world. I went to the University of Kentucky
with Northrop Frye in 1964, for a joint visit in which we
engaged in a public debate much like we are doing right

now (except that he was a much fiercer man than Mike Payne) and we agreed to teach classes as well as engage in these combats; well, the people at Kentucky asked 'What would you like to do?', and then they said to me 'You'd better do the Shakespeare class,' so Frye said 'What shall I do?' and they said 'You do the Northrop Frye course.' He was so important in those days, as were several others. Look at Kenneth Burke, for example; a theorist, if ever there was one, but now a forgotten theorist, virtually. Then there is Leavis, who was so immensely powerful, in an odd sort of way in the institution, and indeed the New Critics, who are now despised, I think unjustly for the most part. All these people were alive and kicking, some of them still are perhaps; certainly, Cleanth Brooks was around until only about five or six years ago – indeed, he outlived his reputation. He often spoke of it; it was such a remarkable thing, to have had a career like his, which made him rich, for one thing, but also made him famous, and then made him, before he was dead, forgotten. So, we have these people who propose a way of remodelling the institution, and win great support, many disciples, and then simply disappear.

Well, it may be that post-1968 developments – 1968 was the watershed, I suppose – have been so enormous, and have required such, more or less compulsory, assent from people who take up the profession, that they won't be removed as easily as a single reputation is removed. But all I'm arguing is that it is worth taking a slightly longer view, and thinking that a contraction of some kind in the empire of theory, even if it isn't death, is certainly going to happen. What it will be, of course, it would be foolish to try and predict. But my own, strengthening view – though it's not something that I think I've ever argued at any great length – is that it's important to keep contact between the institution and an educated public, and some of the things that I've tried to do have been in the interests of that. Mike Payne mentioned the Modern Masters series; more recently, and more pleasurably for me, has been the *London Review of Books*, which seems to me to make that match as well as it's being made anywhere – not by my efforts, but by the efforts of the people who actually took it up and ran with it when we got it started. All that kind of work seems to me very important, because it's important to the general civility; I know this was Trilling's argument, another critic no longer respected. Trilling was always talking about 'keeping the road open', keeping some sort of contact between the specialists in the institution and the people outside – the doctors, the lawyers or whatever they may be, educated people with an intelligible and justifiable interest in letters. So, how do you keep that road open? Well, I think something like the *London Review of Books* is an answer to that. My own feeling about my own work is that my Shakespeare book,[3] which I should have written twenty years ago – not now, not in my present old age – when it might have been very much better, is also an attempt at writing for both academics and the general reader; but it's very difficult to hold that kind of approach together, and I don't think it really succeeded. And it may be, of course, that you find yourself in a no man's land between the institution and a wider public, and that you just get shot at; mind you, I've not been particularly bullied about it.

Whatever, it comes to me sometimes that it's time I stopped, that the long historical process which will be involved in the evolution of theory, and the maintenance of something which is still sometimes called literature, is what needs to be studied. However, we'll no doubt find more details to go into in a moment.

Michael Payne: You mention that the concept of literature as we now have it goes back to the eighteenth century; but looking up, say, Samuel Johnson's definition of literature in the great Dictionary, he has a very eclectic definition; I believe at one point there he says 'Learning'. Now, such a definition of literature as that, I might say, would encompass the theoretical revolution, including much of the critical work that you have done yourself, but literary value, as I understand it, is, for you, an 'other' to theory in some ways, is it not? What do you mean by literary value?

Frank Kermode: Well, there is no suggestion that questions of literary value should be given immunity from theoretical discussion; on the contrary, it seems to me a central issue in literary theory, or aesthetic theory, of course. I think we've suffered a bit from the condemnation of the aesthetic as an ideology, which, of course, is a very strong tendency. I don't believe that is necessary; I believe that it may mistakenly be taken to be so, but it doesn't seem to me to follow essentially from that.

I've been very struck recently by an article which appeared in a journal I used to admire, namely *Critical Inquiry*, which I don't admire any more, but which had a long article by Mary Poovey.[4] Poovey, who is obviously a very intelligent scholar, argues that the concept of organic unity, which has been totally exiled from literary theory in recent years, is actually the groundwork for all modern theoretical approaches to literature, still. Organic unity used, of course, to be regarded as one of the hallmarks of integrity and value in any work of art; it was believed that a proper work of art had a certain kind of coherence which, by analogy, could be compared to biological structures. If you look at volume eight of the *Cambridge History of Literary Criticism*, on the very first page it says that there's been a great divide in recent criticism, that the concept of organic unity lies well to the other side of the divide, and we have no interest in this concept any more. In fact, in the entire volume, eight hundred pages, or so, you will not find any discussion of anything resembling that. You'll find it discussed as a historical issue, in relation to Schlegel or Coleridge and so on, but despite its vital importance to such as Henry James, you won't find any notion that there must be a coherence which is far beyond the mere assembly of related facts, that there is something which, in fact, we judge value by, and that one of the criteria would be organic wholeness. So it's very interesting to have this argument made by someone who, I think, would wish to be identified with theory rather than with old criticism; what Poovey argues, in effect, is that this ghost – organic unity – is still haunting a lot of theorists, and it may, therefore, turn out to be a valuable concept.

The organic concept, or analogy – all these concepts are analogies, really – was very strong among the German Romantics; they actually go on to say not only that the *coherence* of an object, the relevance of all the parts to the whole, resembles a plant, or some other biological unit, but the fact that the object *decays*: they even allow for the decay of organic stuffs. And that spreads to the analogy when it is applied to poems and so on – they too decay. One of the things which would determine a lack of value in an artistic product would be precisely the failure of the parts to submit to the whole, which would be an indication that it was about to fall apart. Clearly, you can't work that analogy forever, but it's in Aristotle – Aristotle doesn't say it's like a plant, but he says that there are wholes; he's trying to define what wholes are, and he says they are those in which the parts cohere. He keeps away from saying 'like an animal', as far as I can remember, but still, he's interested in the idea of wholeness, and wholeness suggests a doctrine of autonomy, or an autotelic doctrine that does actually insist that 'this is different' in that it is part of a consistent whole. Unlike the discourse going on around about it, from which it draws many of its elements, the work of art *can* be constituted as something that resembles a biological organ. That would be one of the distinguishing marks; it would be an index of value. You might say it's not a good index, in the sense that it depends on a shaky analogy, but there you are, that's the position we're in.

Michael Payne: In an aside, just a moment ago, you offered an interpretation of the title of this conference; I think you said something like 'it's about death'. One could certainly read 'life after theory' differently than being about the death of theory – is this wishful thinking on your part?

Frank Kermode: No, I thought I made it clear, I don't at all wish harm to anybody. I guess it depends upon what you mean? What sort of life after theory do you have in mind? Heaven, I suppose.

Michael Payne: Let me put it another way. I'm not, obviously, characterizing *your* work, or your critique of theory, which I think has been marked by civility (and that's a part of your own language), but there's been a lot of hatred of theory. I recall, for example, a cover of the *London Review of Books* that included a review of a book by Louis Althusser, and it was a full-page photograph of Althusser with the title, 'The Paris Strangler'.[5] There was also an ongoing discussion in the *TLS* recently about whether Foucault's particularly 'perverse' notion of truth led him to infect all kinds of young boys with AIDS, and that discussion – a pointless and stupid discussion, I thought – went on for issue after issue. I'm not trying to criticize these specific instances, but just to suggest that perhaps they're symptoms of an ongoing hatred of theory, and I wonder if you have any thoughts about where that hatred comes from, if you think it's there.

Frank Kermode: I don't know. It is true that Karl Miller, when he was editing the *LRB*, had a strong dislike of theory. He'd put unfetching photographs of Foucault on the cover, and that kind of thing; he didn't like it. On the other hand, it was represented, it was discussed, though perhaps too often by people who didn't entirely agree with it. It's been different, I think, in more recent years; there is, I think, now no animus against theory; mind you, it doesn't very often get discussed, that's true. Anyway, the issue is not the policy of the *London Review of Books*, I suppose, it's more whether there is a hatred of theory. Well, there is, of course; but there's a hatred of many things in the world, why should theory be exempted? There's a hatred of religion; what do you conclude from that? Would you expect any movement *not* to have its detractors? After all, theory has taken control of what is by now a very large, though impotent, institution: namely, the study of Literature; in America, for example, the Modern Language Association has around 25,000 members – most of them involved, somehow, in theory. Well, if you think of that, it's not surprising that there are people who don't like them, who find reasons for disliking them, which are not all bad reasons. There's a nice little book, by a man called Mark Bauerlein, in which he gives a list of certain expressions which recur in modern theoretical discussion;[6] he simply asks what they mean, and whether the people who are using them have any idea what they mean, or whether there isn't a kind of bandwagon of jargon terms which people help themselves to (apologies for the mixed metaphor) and coast along simply by using this language. He talks about terms like 'construction', for example, which is very often used without any sense of the intellectual history of that term. Other people have noticed, including myself, the tendency to take a free ride on certain aspects of the terminology that is now current in the field. It doesn't really involve a great deal of serious thinking, it just involves knowing these words and putting them together. So, that would be one reason, I think, why you might find people who actually do attack certain aspects of theory, but who cannot be said to have a blanket hatred for it. That would be too strong.

Michael Payne: I'd rather not have *you* take a free ride on the phrase, 'literary value', so I'd like to nibble at that a little bit more, if I may. You mention the Modern Language Association, and in a prize-winning essay in the PMLA not too long ago, Jeffrey Nealon, announced (I'm not sure what the tone is, whether he's proud of this, or sad) that 'deconstruction in most English departments now is dead'.[7] Do you think so?

Frank Kermode: Well, how would I know, I don't know many English departments. I wouldn't be surprised if it had slackened a bit, it is what you would expect, I think. The other cases, Foucault, for example, got a tremendous boost from the support of the New Historicists, some of whom are very good and interesting, so you get uneven developments from one or the other. Maybe the fact that Derrida, for example, has been a very celebrated person as well as a celebrated writer, as it were, for something like forty years now, maybe that's enough, you know. Maybe it all slows down after that; we live in a celebrity culture, as everybody keeps saying, and Jacques Derrida is a celebrity.

Michael Payne: Is there a possibility, though, that certain theoretical protocols, or certain protocols of reading become normalized in the profession? And that they don't go away, they don't die out, but they simply become a part of the way in which literary interpretation, or reading happens?

Frank Kermode: Could you give an example of such a protocol?

Michael Payne: Well, I tried to. I tried to sneakily suggest that you were practising deconstruction back in 1952 and 1954, in the introductions to your book on pastoral, and your edition of *The Tempest*, and it's right there in your reading of Bushy's speech to the Queen.

Frank Kermode: Going back to that prehistoric piece from 1952 – then I think the strongest influence on me was William Empson. Now, Empson is an interesting case here, because, although he hated theorists, especially modern theorists (in fact he called Derrida 'Nerrida' for some reason, he couldn't get his name right even),[8] in his earlier days Empson was a considerable theorist. I mean, he was rejected for that; *The Structure of Complex Words,* which came out in 1951, he rightly thought a great book, his greatest achievement, and the opening chapters of that book are incredibly theoretical, and very original, but nobody paid any attention to them. The only person I ever came across who admired and was willing to discuss them in detail was John Holloway, who was interested in all varieties of what was then modern criticism. So, Empson is another instance, if one more were needed, to show that people of the utmost brilliance and power who decide to join our world can be totally rejected; I may be wrong to say it, but I see no evidence of keen interest in Empson any more, whether in his verse or in his criticism. But he had a strong idea, a strong commitment to the idea of value. His idea of great poetry was John Donne, of course; I think he had mistaken ideas about Donne (that's another point) – but what he felt and went on feeling was the sheer excitement of Donne's poems. If you'd said 'there's a real difficulty about literary value', Empson's reply would have been 'well, I'm not going to talk to you then, you're not worth talking to' – that would have been his response. He would never have read a book like Barbara Herrnstein Smith's book, *Contingencies of Value* (1988) – he should have done, because it's a very interesting book, which goes into the question of not just how works of art are valued, but how anything is valued, whether it's precious stones, or clothes or whatever it might be; it's a very tricky and interesting subject and, as far as I know, it's alone in that field.

Michael Payne: Let me ask you one last question, and then we'll get things open for others from the floor. One institution that I think you've had an admiration for throughout your whole professional life (and I think it's still there, but I'm not sure, and I'm asking you to correct this) is the Warburg Institute in London; now, of course, Aby Warburg's papers are published, and so we can get a better idea of what was going on there at the Warburg Institute when it was still in Hamburg. As we know, he was very interested in visual marks of culture, and thus amassed this huge photographic collection and so on, in order to study the culture of the Renaissance. Do you think there was a theoretical investment there in Aby Warburg's project, going all the way back to the pre-London years?

Frank Kermode: Well yes, for sure, there was. The Warburg Institute is my idea of scholarly heaven, actually – not quite so heavenly as it used to be when you were allowed to smoke in the stacks, but it's still pretty perfect. I don't have a lot to do with it now, but when I was young I did, because I was then working in areas where it could be helpful. It has the most amazing library, which, of course, still follows the design of Warburg himself. The basic idea in his own work, which is very well explained by Gombrich in the official biography of Warburg, was that there is a kind of afterlife of ancient objects and ideas. So you can illustrate this with a picture library; you can show how a figure on a sarcophagus crops up in a Vyella ad in the 1930s as a kind of ghostly figure of a maenad, the history of which can be traced through to Botticelli and beyond. All that kind of work was behind the creation of this extraordinary library, and extraordinary photographic collection. Warburg's theory of a library was that it should enable you to find not the book that you are looking for, but the book that you need, and this is expressed in a whole series of elaborate colour codes. You have to be pretty smart to understand how to use it – I simply used to tail along behind Joe Trapp and do what he told me, and I'd always find what I needed, not what I wanted. In addition, that was such an intense concentration of genuine and original and exciting scholarship, with figures like Frances Yates and Perkin Walker, for example, who were quite remarkable people – there they were in adjacent studies, doing things that would seem to me quite beyond the ordinary powers of human beings. For example, Frances, if she heard there was a book in Hungarian that she needed for her purposes, she'd go and learn Hungarian; she'd learn languages in order to read a particular book; and then, of course, she had such originality, and such an exciting mind – a sometimes overexcited mind, I dare say, as in some of the business about the theatre, and about the Valois tapestries. All these things made of historical scholarship an amazing adventure, which was very exciting for young people like me back in the forties. And that's why I loved it, and still do; it's the only scholarly institution to which I actually give money, in fact. I do admire it very much, though I never go in there, now; now all the old people have actually died or retired – there are a lot of very bright young people, but they don't know me, so I don't go in. So, yes, for an institute of historical study, not primarily of literature of course, mostly of the visual arts, and ideas like magic, and so on, the Warburg Institute is my model.

Anon: Sir Frank, do you remember the 1970s World Books series of articles which you wrote? You wrote one about the writer, Henry Green, and I just wanted to ask you – bearing in mind these articles were about thirty or so years ago – does what's happened to the reputation of Henry Green since relate at all to what you've had to say about literary value?

Frank Kermode: This is really a question of the market, and fashion, isn't it? There are always novelists who never quite make it into unquestioned esteem – like Ford Madox Ford, for example, who is always on the threshold. Green is a difficult case because he's so contemptuous of a readership. I greatly admire many of his books (perhaps not the late ones, but the early ones) but I can easily understand why some people don't. Take a book like *Party Going*, for example, which I have written quite a lot about; it is possible to read that book without having the faintest idea what it's about, and I think that the novel-reading public don't, on the whole, care for that; so when the reader needs to have a critic who's attuned himself or herself to that particular kind of writing – to tell you why to like it – I think that's what people don't go in for. I think *Loving* is a beautiful novel but I can well understand that some people say 'it's self-indulgent'. So there are all sorts of reasons why people stay in and drop out of favour (mostly the latter, I suppose); I think the same is probably true of Graham Greene, I don't think people bother much about him anymore. And there are novelists – very good novelists – like Arnold Bennett, who is still somewhat despised because Henry James didn't like him. The business of reputations creates difficult problems, because you have to think: 'well, if you're so sure that Bennett's novel, *Riceyman Steps*, for example, is worthy to be thought of as one of the best twentieth-century novels in English (which I think it is) you've got to say *why*' – it's no use saying 'people are wrong to neglect *Riceyman Steps*'. Give them a reason for *not* neglecting it; that's the hard part of criticism, I think – it's in a sense a creation of value; it's the imposing of a valuation (which is what value is about). Are we getting there?

Michael Payne: We are.

Gary Day: I was wondering if part of the problem of defining literary value lies in the fact that the unconventional literary text is always going to *re*define literary value. So do you think, firstly, that part of literary value is in founding a new sense of value? And, secondly, do you think that literary value has become a more acute problem recently – partly because it was ignored by 'theory' and partly because we live in an audit culture where value is supposed to be transparent and quantifiable?

Frank Kermode: I think I agree with the implied answers to your questions. No doubt you could argue that the creation of literary value depends upon what people say about a particular thing; I mean, it's very difficult to maintain that something is of great value if it is never mentioned by anybody; there has to be a kind of chorus of people talking about the book in question. Take a particular instance: take the case of *Ulysses*. *Ulysses* was obviously going to distress people who had conventional criteria for judging the value of a novel; a lot of preparation was done for its acceptance as a novel, by Eliot and others – *Ulysses* was quite a famous book *before* it appeared because of all the kind of advance publicity that was drummed up. Then, of course, it got the publicity of being banned, which is always good for a book; and then, once it came out, there was a steady drumbeat of praise, analysis and so on, so that now everybody – pretty well everybody – would include it among the most important novels of its age. But if, in fact, it had been printed in Paris in a limited edition, and it didn't have important people (like Eliot) who ran journals writing about it, *Ulysses* might just have sunk. There's no magic about this, I think; value is in the real world, in the sense that it's part of the world of publicity. A bad book could, presumably, be exalted in very much the same way; I mean, look at Leavis's famous remark about the Sitwells being not part of the history of literature, but part of the history of publicity. It's kind of right – they don't get any publicity anymore, so they've more or less disappeared. This is how canons are preserved; they're only preserved because people keep talking about them. Books die if they're not talked about – this is a highly pragmatic view of the matter, but I think this is true.

Herman Rapaport: I would suggest that we are in a rather peculiar situation in which on the one hand one gets a sense that theory is dominant and on the other hand the sense that there is a lack of theory across the curriculum – though some colleagues use it, many others do not. Indeed, among many there is always a desire for theory to go away, a kind of death wish. I find this a peculiar dynamic.

Frank Kermode: Well, perhaps I've misrepresented the picture by saying that the institutions are now being totally absorbed by theory; this is not true, obviously it's overstated. But I have to think that even the people who are doing what you think they should not be doing, or not doing what they ought to be doing, are theorists in their way; as Mike Payne was suggesting, even in the dark ages back in the 1950s, people were making remarks that had a theoretical bearing. And this must be true; you can't continue to discuss music, or painting or literature, without actually assuming certain theoretical positions, even if you don't state them clearly. So really, what I am struggling to get round to, is that this is more a struggle between two theories, one of which is highly developed, or much more highly developed than the other. As I tried to say at the beginning, I myself have no objection to that; you *must* allow that thinking about how you think when you are thinking about literature is an important thing to do. It should not, however, be the only thing that one does – I think that is really the gravamen of what I was saying in the earlier part of the morning.

Mike Tintner: Listening today only confirms my view that those in the academy have no theory, or philosophy to account for what makes a good work of art. For instance, you don't have a way to distinguish between popular art and high art; you have talked about organic unity but I would suggest that the Hollywood film is more organically unified than Shakespeare. Your theories just cannot explain why the canon exists. I would say that the first thing you should be saying when you study literature is 'we just don't know what we're doing'. The reality is confusion isn't it?

Frank Kermode: I think the Hollywood point is an interesting one, but it was foreseen by the Romantic theorists with their very firm distinction between mechanical and organic form, and they would no doubt give your Hollywood picture a diploma for excellent mechanical form but they would certainly want to distinguish it from Shakespeare. These were or are the tools and, as you say, they don't really bear very close inspection; I mean, once you begin to look at organicism, you see that an incredible amount has been invested in a very shaky firm, really, and this would be true of a lot of theoretical positions; this is the point you made. The fact that we're confused is true; I don't think we can contest that, I think we're all in a terrible muddle, but we shouldn't cease from trying to reduce the confusion. It may be that there's something benign about being confused in the face of what seem to be really important 'statements' – though they're not exactly statements – about human life, or the human mind and how it can produce a great painting or a great poem. I think all these things matter very much to us; in fact, it's even a literary theoretical point which belongs to I. A. Richards, I suppose, that the whole point of works of art is that they *reduce* confusion. Theory may not reduce confusion, but works of art do reduce confusion – he says 'they reorganize your impulses'. Richards's psychology is completely out of the door today, so we have to find other ways of saying that art and literature are good for you. But we'll come up with some of them someday.

Michael Payne: Since we're very close to being on the verge of defining literary value, this is probably a good time to stop, so thank you very much.

3

truth after theory
Christopher Norris

Michael Payne: As a way into this conversation with Christopher Norris, I offer you, rather abruptly, a short list of what I hope you'll find provocative propositions.

No. 1: Recent developments in cultural and critical theory are not limited in their significance or appeal to a small section of the academic community; instead they both reflect, and impact on, wider cultural, political and social spheres of activity. Because its language is performative, theory incurs important ethical responsibilities that we ignore at our peril.

No. 2: The last two decades have witnessed Western political corruption on a grand scale, in which Parliamentary and Congressional opposition has had little effect; the activist opposition that has occurred, however, has often resorted to suspect forms of critical analysis and debate. The result has been a terminal breakdown in the structures and values of democratic accountability.

No. 3: Leftist intellectuals have promoted an ethos of cynicism, both within and outside the academy, often under the label of postmodernism; a cynicism that has acquiesced in the levelling of the distinctions between truth and falsehood, principle and dogma, civil democracy and consumer choice.

No. 4: Theory has consequences, although there have been decadent efforts to deny them, whether in the name of professional gamesmanship (Stanley Fish) or outrageously disengaged intellectual fashion display (Jean Baudrillard).

No. 5: 'Theory-talk' has even subtler negative consequences in the way it may seduce students, and others, into disregarding the difference between scepticism and cynicism, and to forget that truth is the ultimate prize of critique.

No. 6: One of the things that makes it especially difficult to reclaim truth after theory is that many of its advocates unwittingly, or with faint heart, or by hyperbole or out of ubiquitous human frailty, have tarnished theory and truth, or cheapened it, or made its name suspect. Some examples of these: Hayden White, on history as narrative fiction; Richard Rorty, on philosophy as a kind of writing; Stanley Fish, on law as a rhetorical activity; Paul de Man, on the epistemology of tropes; Wittgenstein, on the claim that 'the limits of my language are the limits of my world'; and careless readers of Nietzsche everywhere.

No. 7: If it were ever actually believed that the greatest legacy of the European Enlightenment was the capacity of critical reason to make the world better, such faith is now in tatters, undermined from within and without, but most immediately vulnerable to the treason of intellectuals, or theorists. Perhaps all of us in the wake of Nietzsche share some of the blame for the eclipse of the value of truth.

Although I may have gotten a bit carried away with number seven, the other propositions stay close to the language of Christopher Norris's writings during the last decade, and in fact all of the first six propositions are derived from a single text, the great polemical introduction to his book, *Reclaiming Truth*. Because Chris writes faster than I can read, I have found the last few months most welcome as an occasion to try to fill in the gaps of what I've read of his books since I last had the pleasure of surveying his publications for a preface to his book, entitled *Spinoza and the Origins of Modern Critical Theory*, published in 1991. I won't risk giving an inaccurate number of books he's published since then but I can't avoid mentioning that he had a miracle year in 1997, when three books appeared – exactly thirty years after Derrida's miracle year – among them was *Resources of Realism*, which was dedicated to Frank Kermode.

There are a couple of pages in Chris's book on Derrida in the Modern Masters series, that seem to me some of the best pages that he has written, and they seem also to herald his determination to recover truth from theory's sometimes ludicrous excesses, insofar as it can be recovered. He begins by asking, in effect, what happens when philosophical texts are read anti-mimetically, as Derrida does in *The Double Session*. 'To read this way,' Norris writes, 'would involve the most scrupulous attention to those moments of stress in the philosophic text where writing perceptibly exceeds and disturbs the order of *mimesis*, of presence, and origins. At such points, the discourse of philosophy is shadowed by a mimic writing, whose effect is the obverse of everything envisioned in Socrates' model of speech as the authentic unveiling of truth.'[1] As Chris Norris proceeds to read this way, he is exploring that subtle, but inescapable and fundamental distinction between truth as mimesis, and truth as *aletheia*. The first, mimesis, is the distinctly referential idea of truth as an adequate matching-up, a correspondence between words and the things they can properly be used to represent. The second, *aletheia*, he describes this way:

> there is a higher reality of essences, 'forms' or ideas, which are locally embodied in the things we perceive but which can only be *known* in their essential nature through a process of inward seeking-after-truth. This is the concept of truth as *aletheia*, as the moment of epiphany, or inward 'unveiling', vouchsafed to the soul through an exercise of reason transcending all forms of sensory perception. And it is the unique authority of Socrates' teaching – a teaching conducted exclusively through dialogue, through the *spoken word*, without recourse to the bad art of writing – that enables this truth to take hold in the minds of his genuine disciples.[2]

The neglect of this distinction between truth as mimesis and truth as *aletheia* has led to serious problems in teaching and writing about theory. Indeed, it may give rise to a fundamental distinction between post-modernism and poststructuralism. It seems to me that one of Christopher Norris's most sustained commitments has been to return us to truth; especially here, truth in its multiplicity.

So, Chris, would you like to start by showing how I've completely misread you?

Christopher Norris: No, I'm very grateful, in fact quite overwhelmed. Empson wrote a Postscript to that early book of mine and said that he ended up wondering whether his work deserved so much devoted scrutiny. I feel rather the same, and with a lot more reason than Empson. Still, you've put me in an awkward spot – I'm sure without meaning to – because I wrote those sentences (and many others like them) a good few years ago and am not too keen to have them quoted back at me two decades on!

Well, it's true, I suppose I've been banging on about truth for a good while now, as in that particular passage where I was trying to sort out just what Derrida meant by truth. For some time I've been trying to defend not just a 'version' of Derrida, but – to use some quaint terminology – a faithful, or responsible reading of Derrida, one that would go against both the postmodernist appropriations of his work and an 'ethics of deconstruction' that seems to me philosophically and ethically unintelligible. You might say it has been a kind of rearguard action, an attempt to retrieve what I think is most important about Derrida's work, in particular his early work, texts such as *Of Grammatology*, *Dissemination*, *Writing and Difference* and *Margins of Philosophy*. Also no doubt it has something to do with my own intellectual autobiography, if that doesn't sound too pompous; with the fact that I was brought up on those early texts of Derrida, which I came across mainly through the happy chance of attending Frank Kermode's seminars at University College, London way back in the early 1970s.

I suppose I'd want to stress that Derrida's early works are *philosophical* works, not just in the sense that they are 'about' philosophy but also in the sense that they are intensely concerned with issues of truth, representation and mimesis, as in the case of the essay on Mallarmé and Plato from *Dissemination;* moreover, they are argued in a very careful, meticulous and logical way. Of course, Derrida is generally regarded, at least by analytic philosophers, as being a rather zany, maverick, 'literary' thinker, one who doesn't stick by the rules of rational and 'serious' argument. I think, on the contrary, that if you go back to the early texts you find a first-rate detailed explication of certain anomalies, aporias and logical complications in Plato, Aristotle, Hegel, Husserl, Lévi-Strauss and others. They are, then, exemplary *philosophical* texts, and in a sense that most analytic philosophers, if only they could be persuaded to read Derrida, or to read him without prejudice, could be brought to recognize. A part of my project, I guess, is to reclaim Derrida from the large number of mostly 'literary' commentators who've read him in a very different way. Now, I'd have to concede that some of Derrida's more recent work would have to be read as going against some of the claims I'm making for his early work; so of course I have my favourite texts, as, I suppose, do other commentators on Derrida.

So, yes, I have been talking a lot about truth, and also trying to make the connection between what philosophers have to say on this topic – analytic philosophers among them – and the issue of truth as it bears upon questions of moral and political engagement. Academics often seem to have a problem in linking their more specialized interests with their sense of larger, perhaps more urgent socio-political concerns; and trying to do so *does* create a difficult state of mind, not quite schizophrenic, but a dissociated state of mind, and at times (without wishing to sound too melodramatic) a real sense of guilt. The only time I felt that the two things were really coming together was in a book I wrote ten years ago after the Gulf War, in response to Jean Baudrillard's notorious pair of articles: the first said the Gulf War would *not* 'take place' because it would be a kind of media-simulated mass illusion, or hyperreal spectacle, and so we would have no means of knowing for sure whether the Gulf War really *was* taking place; the second article, written after the Gulf War, declared, quite consistently, that it had *not* taken place, and for all the same half-baked reasons. I started out writing a response – just an essay to begin with – and then it became a book with the title *Uncritical Theory: postmodernism, intellectuals, and the Gulf War*, which just about captures the polemical tone and the fact that it was written (partly on coach trips up to anti-war demonstrations in London) in the white heat of moral indignation at what was being done in 'our' name by the US and British governments.

So that was an occasion when the two things did come together, the politics and the broadly philosophical critique of various poststructuralist and postmodernist positions in cultural theory. I wouldn't want to disown anything I wrote in that book, but I suppose that even there there is a certain odd gap between the 'philosophy' and the 'politics', and besides, the theorizing in that book was done very much on the wing. Nevertheless, here and elsewhere I have thought it worthwhile to defend truth, to analyse the various implications of realist and anti-realist approaches, and also – as part of this project – to bridge the perceived gulf between the so-called 'continental' (that is to say, post-Kantian mainland European) tradition and the so-called 'analytic' (post-Frege–Russell, chiefly Anglo-American) line of descent. One of the most striking things here is that there are positions on the analytic side, pretty extreme anti-realist positions, which, if you follow through their consequences, in terms, say, of historical understanding, are just as extreme as some of the postmodernist positions.

Take for instance Michael Dummett who's a very respectable, highly esteemed analytic philosopher, but one who has convinced himself partly on logical grounds, and partly on grounds deriving from his reading of Wittgenstein, that it doesn't make sense to say that there are any objective truths, let's say about past events, beyond those that we can establish by the best methods of historical inquiry. In the same way, there are no mathematical truths beyond those for which we possess an adequate proof procedure; and there are no truths generally, except those which we can find out, verify, prove or ascertain by some method at our current or (maybe) our future disposal. So we can make various historical statements – like 'George W. Bush misread the autocue six times while practising his inaugural speech', or 'Margaret Thatcher smiled imperceptibly as she ordered the sinking of the *General Belgrano*' – which of course can't be verified (or falsified) since we have no eyewitness evidence and which therefore, according to Dummett, are neither true nor false. Now realists would want to say, 'well, these statements are objectively true or false, they have to do with the way things actually were'. Dummett would say, 'no, if there's no eyewitness account or no documentary means of proof, then there is no truth of the matter, aside from this question of the scope and limits of our knowledge'. Now this is a very respectable, in fact a widely influential, position within analytic philosophy; however, it seems to me flat wrong, indeed philosophically perverse, but explaining just *why* it's wrong, and putting up arguments against it, is a difficult and fairly technical kind of business.

The point I'm making is that, in a sense, my interests have gone off in a different direction, and I'm now writing what might seem – at least to literary and cultural theorists – books of a rather dry, analytical, politically disengaged sort. But I think there is a real connection to be made between these issues in philosophy of mathematics, logic and language and other, really quite urgent historical or socio-political issues about truth and falsehood. You can see this when Dummett (who is a good left-liberal with strong credentials in working for better race relations) frets intermittently about the kinds of consequence his anti-realist position might have if applied, say, to the claims of right-wing 'revisionist' historiographers or – at the limit – Holocaust-deniers. I suppose this is another example of what I was talking about earlier, that is, the problem that many academics have in squaring their more professional interests with their wider social and political concerns.

Indeed this goes back to the point Mike Payne made about Hayden White and the various things I have written about the uses and abuses of postmodern–sceptical historiography. This doesn't apply so much to White's earliest, I think best book, *Metahistory*, where he's making the quite reasonable point that when we read different historians who are nominally discussing 'the same' event – let's say, four nineteenth-century German historians – they can all be seen to give very different versions of that event, according to their ideological *parti pris*. That is, they deploy different kinds of narrative emplotment and different rhetorical figures (the famous four: metaphor, metonymy, synecdoche, irony) whose relative prominence in any given case will quite decisively influence our understanding of the events in question. This tells us a lot about historio-graphy, about the way that history gets written, what gets included, what gets omitted, what gets played up or played down. So there is certainly a place for narra-tive analysis, or for textual and rhetorical analysis, as a distinct and reputable branch of historiographic inquiry. But at this stage – as I read him – White is not saying that history is ultimately a textual construct, or a kind of backward rhetorical projection, a 'history of the present', as Foucault proclaimed, with more than a nod toward Nietzsche's sceptical genealogies of power/ knowledge. White is not denying the existence of historical truths but pointing out that our only access to them is through these variously formed narrative modes of emplotment.

Later on, though, White does go much further in a sceptical, or Nietzschean direction, toward the radically constructivist view that *history itself*, what 'actually' happened, is ultimately a product of the way we tell it from various narrative perspectives. In other words he tends to let go of the distinction between *res gestae* and *historia rerum gestarum*, or history in the sense of 'that which happened' and history in the sense of 'that which has been written concerning what happened'. Of course I am not suggesting that White's and Dummett's arguments with respect to history are just flip sides of the same anti-realist coin. They have very different sources – Frege and Wittgenstein in Dummett's case, structuralism and poststructuralism in White's – and they involve very different kinds of criteria. Still it is worth remarking on the points of convergence between them and the extent to which anti-realism has taken hold within both traditions of thought.

So, from various angles, you're getting this convergence of sceptical, anti-realist, or strong constructivist views, and you can find it in philosophy of language and logic, mathematics, philosophy of history and – not least – in philosophy of science. Here it comes mainly from the influence of Kuhnian thinking about paradigm–relativism and the idea that scientists with different theories must be thought to inhabit different worlds. There's a great debate about just how literally we are meant to interpret that claim, but a lot of Kuhn's readers have taken it at face value, and drawn some pretty extreme relativist conclusions. So, where Aristotle witnessed a swinging stone seeking out its 'natural place' in the order of the elements, Galileo witnessed the gravitationally induced movement of a pendulum. However it is begging the question – so Kuhn argues – to speak of both parties as witnessing 'the same' phenomenon in either case. Rather we should think of Aristotle's 'world' as one in which matter could indeed be observed to seek out its natural place in the order of the elements and Galileo's 'world' as one which contained such objects as pendulums whose motion was explained by the law of gravity. Above all, we should not allow our understanding to be swayed by the stock idea that Galileo (not Aristotle) got it right. What this case demonstrates, rather, is the lack of any common criteria – of truth, reference, predictive warrant, observational accuracy, etc. – that would give a handle for comparing two episodes in the history of science.

So, from that quarter, and from various others – such as social constructivism or Foucault's Nietzschean genealogy of knowledge – there emerged this sceptical-relativist trend that rapidly colonized large areas of 'advanced' thinking in the human and social sciences. I'm not saying that these developments were wholly disastrous, or that they didn't produce some interesting and valuable work. But the trouble with a lot of these debates in 'theory' is that positions get polarized, with people taking a Manichaean view, and so you'll find postmodernists saying that any appeal to truth is a kind of coercive or totalitarian ploy, an attempt to silence dissident or opposing beliefs. Hence the idea that the Enlightenment, deeply attached as it was to notions of critical reason, progress and the liberating power of knowledge, inevitably turned into a repressive or 'totalizing' movement of thought – and 'totalizing' becomes one of the most insulting words you can use. I remember going to a conference at Illinois [University] way back in 1983 where Fredric Jameson was delivering the final lecture, and some women at the back started chanting 'you totalizing bastard!' It seemed a rather arcane sort of insult and left me puzzled at the time. But one does get this postmodernist idea of truth as something inherently oppressive, just a stick to beat opposing views. Admittedly – and sometimes, I suppose, I've been guilty of this – you also get views of postmodernism that tend to reduce it to a kind of way-out, addle-brained scepticism. But then, having made this mildly ecumenical gesture, I want to say that there *is* an awful lot of nonsense that nowadays gets passed off as sophisticated wisdom among cultural theorists who don't seem to grasp the philosophical as well as the political implications of what they are saying.

I'm aware of not having answered your last point, the one about problems in teaching the distinction between truth as *mimesis* and truth as *aletheia*. I agree that there is a lot of confusion here, and it often comes out in a strain of Heidegger-influenced talk about the 'end of philosophy', or at any rate the end of a certain way of thinking – the representational paradigm – which conceives truth in terms of correspondence, of Aristotelian *homoiosis*, or *adaequatio*. So we are supposed to think, after Heidegger, that this is a bankrupt idea, one that belongs to the waning tradition of 'Western metaphysics', and whose effect has been to efface from memory that other, primordial conception of truth as *aletheia*, as authentic 'unconcealment'. Of course, Derrida has himself been much influenced by this *echt-*Heideggerian interpretation of the history of philosophy from Plato to the present, although he does have decided reservations about it. But there are also some analytic (or 'post-analytic') philosophers who argue that the best, perhaps the only way forward from the doldrums of recent logico-linguistic debate is one that takes this Heideggerian turn toward a depth-hermeneutic approach. It often gets joined to a certain understanding of pragmatism, that is to say, by linking up the pragmatist idea of truth as a matter of real-world practical engagement with Heidegger's idea of the 'ready-to-hand', of the tool as the paradigm case of our pre-theoretical involvement with the world. My own view – which I argued in *Resources of Realism* – is that this approach ignores some large problems, partly with Heidegger, partly with pragmatism, and (perhaps most of all) with the strained attempt to bring them out on the same philosophical wavelength. In response to all this I would want to say that the correspondence theory – truth as *homoiosis* – still has a lot going for it and need not be regarded (in Rortian fashion) as the last refuge of old-style philosophers who haven't caught up with the latest conversational rules of the game.

Michael Payne: In some of your earliest books on deconstruction, *Deconstruction: Theory and Practice*, for example, or *The Deconstructive Turn*, you seem to be writing for some distinctly definable audiences; there was, obviously, the more general audience of people interested in theory, but you also seem to be singling out both a philosophical audience, and a literary critical audience. And you seem to be saying to the people in literature: 'if you're going to be serious about theory, you've got to be more serious about philosophy'; while saying to your philosophical audience: 'you need to be more attentive to the literariness of your language, rather than assuming that the language of philosophy is immune to, say, metaphor'. What I want to ask you is, whether your more recent books on the philosophy of science have any kind of parallel, double audience; for instance, are you saying to philosophers of science, that perhaps they need to be more concerned with the realistic claims of science? And are you saying to the scientists, for example, that they need to be more attentive to the theoretical underpinnings of their work?

Christopher Norris: There's a kind of turning point, really; in *The Deconstructive Turn* (1983) I am very much saying to philosophers: look, if you read the classical texts (and I start with Plato and Descartes and go on to Kant, Husserl, Wittgenstein, Austin and Ryle), if you read them deconstructively, with an eye to metaphors, rhetorical devices, narrative structures and so forth, then you'll get a very different idea of what these philosophers were saying than if you read them in the standard, philosophically approved way. So that was what I thought then, convinced as I was that philosophers just hadn't *read* their canonical texts with anything like an adequate attention to detail. I suppose what happened next was that I read Richard Rorty; or rather, that the implications of Rorty's book, *Philosophy and the Mirror of Nature*, and of his later book, *Consequences of Pragmatism*, really sank in. Then it struck me that this kind of approach to philosophical texts – saying, basically, that all concepts are metaphors, all philosophy is a kind of writing, reason is rhetoric and so forth – really was quite corrosive, and also had untoward implications for our understanding of history. It didn't impugn just the claims of Enlightenment reason (bad enough!), but it really came down to a kind of textualist levelling of all those 'discourses', among them philosophy, history and literature, which would leave one with no kind of critical leverage for opposing, say, right-wing revisionist readings of historical events.

Anyway a couple of years later – in 1985 – I published *The Contest of Faculties* which marked, I suppose, a fairly drastic change in my thinking, drawing on philosophers like Frege and Davidson for alternative philosophical resources. So between those two texts there was a change of mind, especially with regard to Rorty and the whole idea that philosophy is best treated as a 'kind of writing' with no special privilege in matters of epistemological or truth-telling warrant. Sometimes I feel rather bad about this because Rorty is a stimulating thinker and a brilliant stylist and a thoroughly likeable person, as it happens, but it did seem to me that some of these ideas at least needed looking at very critically. If there was a turning point, it came with that book, *The Contest of Faculties*, which has a long and highly critical essay on Rorty.

Beyond that, I suppose, yes, the philosophy of science is one of the areas where a lot of these issues really come home. You can see this even in the newspapers; in the recent 'science wars' controversy, as part of the fallout from the Sokal hoax. I refer, of course, to Sokal's famous spoof article, 'Transgressing the Boundaries: toward a transformational hermeneutics of quantum gravity'. Sokal wrote this article, decked out with lots of references to cultural theory, sociology of science, postmodernist pronouncements about quantum physics and so forth, and somehow managed to get it published – presumably with benefit of peer-group review – in the journal *Social Text*. Then, in the same week, he published a piece in the magazine *Lingua Franca* saying that the whole thing was a hoax, and it showed what idiots the sociologists and cultural theorists were, since they couldn't distinguish genuine from pseudo-science. That is, perhaps, the most dramatic and widely publicized example; but what you often get is a sharp divide between, on the one hand, science warriors like Lewis Wolpert who dismiss any approach from a sociological or cultural-historical angle as so much ignorant or scientifically illiterate twaddle, and on the other hand postmodernists who regard any talk of truth, knowledge, progress or whatever, as some kind of oppressive 'totalitarian' discourse.

This, though, is just a travesty of what really goes on when scientists reflect on the way they work and think. The 'spontaneous philosophy' of most scientists, when you talk to them, is a version of Popperian fallibilism; it's the idea that science doesn't and shouldn't claim to possess the absolute, definitive truth about anything. What it does, rather, is propose bold conjectures, test them against the evidence, and try as hard as possible to falsify them; you can never guarantee that you have the truth about anything in science; it's always possible, even if remotely possible, that some new result will come along to falsify your favourite theory. But the point is, once you've got a falsifying instance or obser-vation, then the theory collapses; so all the old problems about induction and so forth can be got around by adopting this falsificationist approach. And that seems to be what most scientists believe; so the standard postmodernist, cultural-relativist attack on the ideology of science, the so-called 'positivist' ideology, is really aiming at a non-existent target.

But these issues still come up in interesting ways in the philosophy of science, especially in quantum physics. So if you go back to the Sokal article, he doesn't just quote passages from Derrida (quite unfairly and out of con-text, actually) and Irigaray, Kristeva and Latour, but he actually quotes passages from Heisenberg and Bohr, the founding figures in orthodox quantum theory. And this rather complicates his argument because quite a lot of postmodern theorizing comes out of that particular interpretation of quantum theory, one which denies that 'classical' (realist) concepts have any application in the quantum domain since everything is subject to uncertainty, paradox and the limits of precise measurement, etc. If you read Lyotard, for instance, he has a habit of yoking all sorts of vaguely apposite allusions – among them chaos theory, undecidability and the theory-laden character of observation-statements – to this particular interpretation of quantum mechanics, which is still by and large the orthodox interpretation, even though it's deeply problematic. The whole notion of 'postmodern' science, as you find it developed in Lyotard's book *The Postmodern Condition*, derives a large part of its credibility from the idea that cutting-edge physics is irreducibly contradictory, or paradoxical, or 'paralogistic' or whatever.

I'd want, then, to defend a realist philosophy of science, which isn't at all what postmodernists like Lyotard are prone to call a 'positivist' philosophy of science. In fact, positivism in its modern (post-1920) form more often goes along with an anti-realist and at times deeply sceptical outlook which these postmodern thinkers would probably find very much to their taste if they had only read the relevant literature.

Michael Payne: I'd like to ask you a question that I'm not quite sure how to put, because one way to take this question is personally, and I don't mean it so much that way. I want to ask you about disciplinary boundaries and disciplinary identities; and I suppose the personal way to put it is: the last time I interviewed you, you were a professor of English, and you are now a professor of Philosophy. What I'm thinking of here is the end of Stanley Cavell's book, *The Claim of Reason*, where he asks the question: 'can philosophy become literature and still know itself?' He doesn't, by the way, ask the question the other way around – namely: can 'literature become philosophy and still know itself?' Anyway, *my* question is: are these disciplinary boundaries real, since you've recently crossed one? Are there really different epistemes, or paradigms that define the disciplines that we work in?

Christopher Norris: To go back to the first part of your question, there is obviously a sense in which you can read philosophy as literature, in the sense that you read it as much for the style as for substantive points of philosophical argument. One example of this would be Hume; you can read Hume for his irony, as a great stylist, as a writer who invites rhetorical analysis along broadly 'literary' lines. You wouldn't read Kant for that reason; nobody would read Kant for his literary qualities, or Hegel for that matter, or a good many recent analytic philosophers. But there are others one could mention – Nietzsche, Kierkegaard, Wittgenstein, Austin, even Adorno, certainly Walter Benjamin – whom you could read with an eye to their 'literary' style, or at least with your attention primarily fixed on their extraordinary gift for the concise expression of complex ideas. And this also goes for some analytic philosophers, Russell and Quine among them, who write in a way that combines great logical precision with an acute awareness of the rhetorical effect of phrasing, emphasis, idiom and so forth. T. S. Eliot says somewhere that if you want a perfect example of finely honed expository prose then you can do no better than Russell's essay 'On Denoting', which is also (as it happens) one major source of the whole analytic approach to philosophy of language and logic.

So yes, there's a sense – an innocuous sense – in which you can read philosophers in a 'literary' way without for a moment discounting the philosophical significance of what they have to say. But there is also a different, to my mind less acceptable, sense in which you read philosophy as 'literature', or as a 'kind of writing', and deploy this idea as a means of suggesting that really philosophy is – and always has been – just a sub-branch of fiction or poetry, one that managed to pass itself off as something different only by entertaining delusions of epistemological grandeur. This is basically what Rorty does, and what I was doing pretty much in a book like *The Deconstructive Turn*, although I did change my mind – and said so quite explicitly – just a couple of years later. The mistake comes in when you say, like Rorty, that there are no boundaries, there are no distinctions, or there is no such thing as a distinctively 'philosophical' way of thinking or reading, because there are no 'philosophical' texts, except according to the standard division of academic labour. What we have instead – according to Rorty – are more or less interesting, creative, imaginative, mould-breaking texts, and it makes no difference whether these belong to the (so-called) 'natural' or 'human' sciences. That's the way to read philosophy, Rorty thinks: if the great dead philosophers are worth reading at all then it's because they did interesting things rhetorically, or in a narrative way, or because their texts spark all kinds of metaphoric associations and possibilities of creative thinking. But if we think they can be read *as philosophers*, as having written a distinctive kind of text, with its own discipline-specific standards of logical argument, consistency, rigour or whatever, then that's a mistake, it's an old-fashioned and just plain boring way of doing philosophy.

No doubt this has partly to do with Rorty's extreme reaction against the kind of analytic philosophy that he was brought up on, what he came to think of as a very narrow, stifling way of doing philosophy. And it is likely to strike anyone with different interests that the analytic house journals – the places where you really *must* publish if you want to boost your departmental grade in the next round of the Research Assessment Exercise – are mainly given over to just the kind of writing that Rorty finds so utterly detached from wider human concerns. But this doesn't mean that you have to throw over the very idea of getting things right, analysing presuppositions and pointing out fallacies, logical flaws, suppressed premises, conceptual dilemmas, alternative (more precise or rigorous) formulations, etc. In fact this is just what Derrida does in those early texts that I mentioned a few minutes ago, and which I think fully deserve the title 'analytic philosophy' in any but a parochial, professionally narrowed sense of that term. You can see this when Derrida writes about someone like J. L. Austin, who himself came at these topics from a quizzical, detached, ironic point of view, and who clearly appeals to Derrida for just that reason, but whom nobody – except perhaps a few hard-line disciples of Russell or Frege – would think of dismissing as simply not up to the mark in 'analytic' terms.

So yes, there are certain generic distinctions that we do need to hang onto, including the distinction between 'philosophy' and 'literature' (or literary criticism). This goes back to the question we discussed earlier about history and whether you can read historical texts as just another kind of writing on a par with fiction or poetry. Here again the example of Hume comes to mind since, of course, Hume's main reputation during his lifetime was as the writer of a history of Britain, rather than as a philosopher, and there is nowadays a fashion for saying: well, it doesn't really matter how we classify his works because they are all rhetorical (or narrative, or textual or 'literary') constructs and our need for this kind of pigeon-holing is just a product of our current professional interests or way of dividing the disciplinary spectrum.

It is, though, I admit, difficult to resist such a claim in relation to Derrida, writing as he does in a highly self-conscious, reflexive and 'literary' style that puts large obstacles in the way of any reading that claims to get him right on this or that point. This is a particular problem with his later work where the intertextual allusions sometimes produce an almost ventriloquistic effect; in early texts like *Of Grammatology* or *Writing and Difference* there is still a fair amount of free-indirect quotation or *oratio obliqua* but at least you can make a good shot at reconstructing the logic of Derrida's argument. Indeed, just recently I've been trying to do it in a systematic way, taking certain passages from *On Grammatology* where he writes about Rousseau and the 'logic of supplementarity', and seeing how they work out when expressed in formal, symbolic terms. Actually the system that works best – that most adequately captures Derrida's argument – is the system of modal logic with operators for necessity and possibility. What I think you can show is that Derrida is working with precisely these notions and bringing out the conflict in Rousseau's texts between a classical or bivalent logic of truth/ falsehood and a 'deviant' (supplementary) logic that creates all sorts of modal complications for any approach along standard, truth-functional lines.

Some logicians – Graham Priest among them – have started to take an interest in this aspect of Derrida's work, and about time too, after all the accusations (from philosophers like Searle) that his arguments don't make any kind of logical sense. Indeed, there is a poignant irony here since one of Derrida's fiercest detractors has been Ruth Barcan Marcus, the Yale logician who has done more than anyone (at least since C. I. Lewis) to bring modal logic up to date by combining it with the modern, post-Fregean apparatus of quantifiers and predicates. So I take some pleasure in showing how Derrida's reading of Rousseau presupposes the validity of a well-known formula which Marcus was the first to propose.

This approach would be much less revealing if applied to what Derrida's been publishing since around the mid-1980s, when there's often a kind of inspired free-association going on; but even here he is still arguing a case, defending certain theses, opposing others and respecting certain standards of logical consistency and truth. In fact, it was precisely his point *contra* Foucault, in the early essay 'Cogito and the History of Madness', that Foucault had no choice but to make rational sense when writing about the relationship between reason and madness despite his claim to be speaking from a standpoint outside and beyond the norms of post-Cartesian rational discourse. So, I think that, to go back to your original question, you do have to hang on to some of those disciplinary distinctions, since otherwise it's not just the distinction between philosophy and literature that becomes blurred, usually at the expense of philosophy, but the distinction between, for instance, historical and fictional narrative.

This recalls my point about Hayden White; there's an enormous difference between saying that all historical texts have a certain, irreducible narrative dimension, and on the other hand saying that history is itself just a kind of fiction. I think this is a category mistake, a mix-up of otherwise useful distinctions, and that modal logic is one useful means of sorting out the muddles involved. Thus some recent narrative theorists – people like Ruth Ronen and Thomas Pavel – have applied modal logic (or the logic of 'possible worlds') in an effort to get beyond the usual poststructuralist/postmodernist idea that everything, history included, is equally a product of textual or fictive representation. I think that it's possible to address this question by looking at issues of causality, agency, chronology, transworld identity and so forth, and deploying the resources of modal logic to clarify the kinds of distinction that we quite routinely bring to bear when reading different sorts of text.

So my answer would be, not that interdisciplinarity, or the attempt to be interdisciplinary, is a bad thing; but rather that certain crucial distinctions can easily drop out if you adopt the pan-textualist, or Rortian 'strong'-descriptivist view that exhorts us to junk the whole idea that different disciplines involve different kinds of knowledge or orders of truth-claim. I know this will strike some people as thoroughly naive and 'positivist' but they might think again about the implications – not least the political implications – of adopting the alternative view.

Michael Payne: It's always very unfair to have anything from one's doctoral thesis quoted in public, but I want to quote a sentence from yours which was published under the title of *William Empson and the Philosophy of Literary Criticism*, and I intend this as an example. Here's the sentence: 'There is no absolute distinction, no possible demarcation, between what is in the text, and what is produced by the critic's active involvement.' Now that might be a reading coming off Empson's texts, but just taking it at face value for a moment I think it has interesting implications for some of the concepts of truth we've been talking about. Is there a textual truth, I suppose I'm asking?

Christopher Norris: I suppose I'd think twice before committing that sentence to paper now. I was thinking there about Empson, who raises this issue with particular force because he's such a brilliant, and at times maverick reader; and because, once you've read *Seven Types of Ambiguity* (1930), so many of the passages he talks about are transformed almost beyond recognition. But the interesting thing is that by the time of his later book, *The Structure of Complex Words* (1951) – which didn't receive anything like the same *succès de scandale* as *Seven Types* – Empson had changed his mind; in fact he said that *Seven Types*, as he now saw it, had licensed all kinds of over-the-top, ingenious verbal explication, and he often accused American critics of doing that, usually, he thought, with some right-wing political or 'neo-Christian' end in view. Anyway he became very worried about the whole issue of authorial intention, and he thought he had taken a much too liberal position, one that acknowledged too few constraints on the critic's freedom to interpret texts in line with their own ideological agenda.

So in the later book he takes a very different approach that involves quite a complex logico-semantic 'machinery' – Empson's term – designed to explain how language can communicate ideas, beliefs, attitudes, even complicated states of feeling that the author, at whatever 'preconscious' level, wished or intended to communicate. I make no apology for plugging *Complex Words* because it's a really terrific book, of literary criticism as well as philosophy of language and logic, or philosophical semantics. I agree with what Frank was saying this morning; it's a curious and rather discreditable fact that literary theorists over the past four decades have steadfastly ignored this book while chasing after every fashionable theory with an import label attached. Basically Empson is trying to explain how there are certain constraints upon interpretation, which come not from the purely semantic aspect of language, but also from the logico-semantic aspect. He thinks there are certain forms of verbal implication, some of them extremely complex, which constrain interpretation because they belong to the structure of the language, which takes a good deal of historical and philological as well as conceptual and logico-semantic unpacking.

So, in other parts of my book I did make the point that the later Empson stressed the limits of interpretation, and its need to maintain a principled respect for some workable conception of authorial intent. And of course this takes us back to Derrida, since you could say that there are two great divergent schools of Derrida interpretation: there are those who value Derrida, as Rorty does, for the fact that he is a wonderfully inventive, creative, original reader of texts, who can make even 'old' philosophical texts open up and mean all kinds of hitherto unsuspected things; and there are those, like me, who want to say: but look, there is this other side of Derrida's work where he argues his way with a scrupulous attentiveness to the text in hand, with great logical rigour, and with a genuine regard for traditional standards of interpretive fidelity and truth

There's a famous passage in *Of Grammatology* where Derrida addresses this question: he says that interpretation, up to a certain point, has to respect the most traditional protocols of reading and scholarship – without that, and without respect for an author's intention, reading could go off in any direction, a bit like some of Empson's more 'inventive' readings in *Seven Types of Ambiguity*. After all, Derrida spent his philosophically formative years working on Husserl, and Husserl's philosophy is centrally concerned with the issue of intentionality, albeit in a much broader sense of the term. Anyway, Derrida says, without that sort of basic respect for an author's intentions, and for the protocols of scholarly method, no reading could even begin; it is a kind of 'indispensable guard rail' that places certain constraints on the otherwise open-ended 'freeplay' of interpretation. But he then goes on to say that this has only ever been a starting-point for interpretation, and that a deconstructive reading is primarily concerned with the relation between what the author 'commands' and 'does not command' with respect to the meaning of his or her text. Here again I should want to say that *Of Grammatology* is less about 'literary' interpretation than about the logico-semantic complications that arise in the reading of Rousseau, Lévi-Strauss, Saussure and others; that is, about issues that take us outside the old lit.crit. debate about authorial intention, one that began with Wimsatt and Beardsley's 1954 article 'The Intentional Fallacy' and which took a more radical (though not, I think, a more philosophically sophisticated) form in poststructuralist talk about 'the death of the author'.

Anyway, when Derrida writes about the 'logic of supplementarity', this is not some kind of wild, freely inventive, pseudo-logic; it is a rigorously specified *devi-*

ant logic, which Derrida finds everywhere at work in the texts of Rousseau and those who inherit the Rousseauist mystique of nature, origins and 'transparent self-presence in the proximity of the voice'. All of which is a hugely roundabout way of saying: yes, I would want to qualify that sentence now, the one that you quoted from my Empson book, although the context gives me a bit of an excuse for having written it!

Michael Payne: You mentioned the Sokal hoax earlier on; and I found his explanation for the hoax very strange, because it reminded me in some ways of your Gulf War book. What Sokal said was that he had become very anxious as someone on the political left because it seemed that people who shared his politics were thinking about truth and verifiability in such a way that made it absolutely impossible for them to carry out effective politics. It's a strange thing to be a champion of truth and to write a text like the one that he published. Does that surprise you?

Christopher Norris: Well, I don't know, I don't think he was being disingenuous, or downright naive. Where he *did* show real naivety was in not foreseeing that the whole thing would be taken up and used by people on the right as ammunition in their war against the cultural theorists. I think he was also naive in not foreseeing that it would be used to take away funding from programmes in Cultural Studies. I mean, that was the ugliest aspect of the whole Sokal affair – it did have large institutional, financial and (academically speaking at least) socio-political implications. But the whole thing was a very confused episode altogether, partly because, as I was saying, Sokal is a realist about quantum physics, and he rejects the orthodox interpretation. So I suppose his point in including those passages from Bohr and Heisenberg on the side of the orthodox theory was, perhaps, to lump them together with the postmodern theorists, although he has more respect for Bohr and Heisenberg than for the people who breezily cite their ideas without much grasp of the physics and philosophy behind them.

Despite the problems, though, there were some good consequences; I do think it's probably raised standards in some of the cultural studies and cultural theory journals. At least editors have been much more careful about what gets through the evaluation process or past the peer-review system. But it sort of muddied the waters; and the other bad thing about it was that he lumped together quotations from all kinds of sources, some of them, I would say, eminently respectable. For instance, when Derrida cites Gödel's undecidability-proof in a passage of *Dissemination*, he knows what he's talking about, he makes it very clear, if you read that passage in context, that he's not just throwing in an impressive-sounding reference to convince us that he's got some advanced mathematics or philosophy of maths behind him. He really knows what it's all about; after all, he came up through the highest levels of the French educational system, and did a lot of philosophy of logic and mathematics. But in the Sokal article you find Derrida quoted alongside various pretentious, ill-informed or downright clueless pronouncements from a whole range of other sources; so it's very much a scatter-shot, hit-and-miss approach, and to that extent it's much less effective as a piece of satire or polemics.

Mike Tintner: I would like to return to Derrida who, it seems to me, misses one of the major aspects of literature – namely that literature is primarily dialogue. Dialogue, you might say, is the difference between literature and philosophy – that's what separates them, and Derrida misses that.

Christopher Norris: Firstly, Derrida is not a literary critic. It's true he's written about Mallarmé, Joyce, Artaud, Sollers and others; and you could say that he reads philosophers in a 'literary' way, at least in one sense of that highly questionable term. But there is another point here, namely the fact that Derrida *is* a very dialogical writer, and one problem with reading his texts – his late texts especially – is the way that he moves almost imperceptibly between different registers, between, say, passages of 'direct' statement, marked or unmarked quotation, near-verbatim paraphrase, 'free-indirect' style, intertextual allusion, tacit cross-reference and so forth. In his essay 'Of an Apocalyptic Tone Recently Adopted in Philosophy' this imbrication of various 'voices' tends to leave the commentator almost at a loss when it comes to deciding where Derrida stands on the topics under discussion. You can say easily enough what the essay is 'about': it is about Kant's defence of Enlightenment values – the values of rational, democratic, open debate – against the kinds of counter-Enlightenment thinking (or the appeal to 'inner truths' vouchsafed through divine inspiration) represented by opponents like Hamann and Jacobi. These were the illuminati, the mystagogues, the self-professed religious elect, apostles of a voice of conscience within, an apocalyptic tone that brooked no dissent and whose edicts were wholly unbeholden to the standards of public accountability or critical reason. What's more, Kant protested, they spoke in a riddling, obscurantist, quasi-poetic language intended to block access for all but those already attuned to the voice of divine inspiration. Now there is a sense – a fairly obvious sense – in which Derrida's essay is 'about' this particular episode in the history of Enlightenment thought, that is to say, Kant's quarrel with those who rejected the appeal to values of rational consensus and uncoerced critical debate. But there is also a sense in which Derrida is writing about his own situation vis-à-vis those present-day critics of deconstruction – Habermas among them – who accuse him, just as Kant accused the mystagogues, of exploiting an arcane 'literary' style or a kind of 'poetico-meta-phorical abundance' (Habermas's phrase) in order to claim some privileged access to truth denied to the exponents of plain-prose critical reason. This is exactly Habermas's charge against Derrida: that he has renounced the 'philosophical discourse of modernity' by blurring the essential genre-distinction between philosophy and literature, or reason and rhetoric.

Of course this is a travesty of Derrida's thought and one that derives, so far as one can tell, from Habermas's habit of relying on secondary sources – Rorty among them – which unfortunately lend 'philosophical' credence to just such a partial and distorted view of Derrida. But it is hard to make the case that this reading is flat wrong because Derrida's essay does explore such a range of styles, voices, rhetorical strategies and argumentative ploys. At one moment he mimics the style of Hamann, Jacobi and the mystagogues, and at the next moment comes out with ringing declarations about the need to keep faith with the 'vigil' of enlightened critical thought, or the Kantian idea of a *sensus communis* – a rational public sphere – opposed to all such fideist conceptions of meaning and truth. And the whole thing is complicated yet further by Derrida's etymological point about the strange proximity between these positions, that is to say, the fact that religiously inspired talk of 'illumination' bears a curious resemblance to secular talk of 'enlightenment' as the best hope of at last throwing off those old, uncritical habits of thought.

Thus the essay is extremely hard to pin down, or extremely resistant to the kind of reading – my kind of reading, I have to say – that would take it as coming out firmly on Kant's side. Of course it's very tempting to pluck bits out of context, the bits that one happens to approve of, or in my case the passages where Derrida says that enlightenment is not just an option, that the 'lucid vigil' of enlightened thought is a moral and political imperative. All the same you don't know whether he is quoting Kant, or alluding to Kant, or rendering the

Kantian 'position' as just one voice among the medley of competing views. I suppose this is what many people think of as the 'literary' element in Derrida's writing, this enormously complex, intertextual weave of different 'voices' or viewpoints – a weave that is not, by the way, wholly confined to his later work, witness a text like 'Dissemination' (1972).[3] I don't think that this ventriloquism is just evasiveness on Derrida's part, or just a good-willed, vaguely ecumenical desire to see the best in various alternative positions. Rather it is a kind of extreme sensitivity to the way that those positions – his own included – have a tendency to exchange places, to turn out sounding curiously like the kinds of position they oppose. This is what happens, Derrida remarks, when Kant and the defenders of Enlightenment reason themselves take on something of an 'apocalyptic tone', a language of revealed truth or illumination and a shedding of the veils of prejudice

But, to return to your question, it is not unusual for philosophers to write in dialogue form so as to try out various positions against a range of objections, counter-arguments, qualifications and so forth. Plato is the obvious example here, although of course with Plato you usually have a pretty good idea of where he stands since his dialogues mostly give Socrates the last word, or are so constructed as to bring you out – 'you', the compliant reader – in agreement with Socrates' views. Yet there are places in the dialogues, famously, where it doesn't work quite like that, and where you wonder, where perhaps you are meant to wonder, whether Socrates hasn't lost a match.

Think too of Hume, or Berkeley, philosophers who wrote in dialogue form because they wanted to talk readers around from a hostile or dissenting viewpoint, with whatever degree of success. Again, perhaps more to the point, think of Kierkegaard whose life's work – or most of it – was a kind of elaborate fictive construction with multiple viewpoints, pseudonymous narrators, endless techniques of narrative indirection, oblique self-commentary and so forth. Wittgenstein is another example since his later writings – texts like the *Philosophical Investigations* – often take this form of an implicit dialogue between different 'voices' or viewpoints, some which seem to have Wittgenstein's approval, his authorial imprimatur, while others appear to lead us up a false path, to evince some philosophical confusion, or produce some hopeless sceptical impasse. Of course there are commentators, orthodox types, who think they know what Wittgenstein means (where the tacit quote-marks need filling in, so to speak) and who back their claims – understandably enough – by citing just those passages that they find most persuasive, or which they think represent his authentic views. But there are others, among them Derrida-influenced readers of Wittgenstein like Henry Staten, who question this confidently orthodox approach and take it to rest on a selective interpretation, one that misses the sheer complexity and (often) the genuine puzzlement that comes across in Wittgenstein's texts. So I really don't think you can accuse Derrida of being somehow 'unphilosophical', or just a 'literary' stylist. If he uses certain 'literary' techniques – like free-indirect style – that are more often found in fiction then this doesn't mean, any more than it does in Kierkegaard's case, that he has taken Rorty's advice and simply opted out of philosophy.

4

music, religion and art after theory

Frank Kermode and Christopher Norris

Michael Payne: What I've been hearing today, first from Frank Kermode, and now from Chris Norris, are some warnings about literary theory. But the warnings come to us not just in a negative voice, or in a negative tone; there is an assertion, an affirmativeness, here, about literary value and about truth. What I wonder, though, is: are there certain inherent hazards of theory that have left us with any compensating benefits?

Frank Kermode: But that's to speak as if theory had just blown in suddenly; that's not to allow for the fact that there always has been some.

Christopher Norris: Well, we've heard a lot today about the limits of theory, or the disadvantages, or even the threat and the danger of certain kinds of theory. But I suppose someone ought to stick up for theory, and in any case we are all talking about it – even 'doing' it – despite these qualms and misgivings. It happens regularly at conferences nowadays, this idea that the time has passed, that 'theory' has had its day, that we need to move on, and then you get everyone discussing it again and the same issues coming up.

It's a bit like Richard Rorty who has been saying for the last twenty years that he doesn't want to do philosophy any more, at least not the kind of analytic philosophy, the specialized stuff that he once used to do before the light dawned and he became a 'post-philosophical' writer. So now he wants to junk that whole idea of philosophy as a special, 'constructive', truth-seeking enterprise and throw in his lot with the literary critics, with 'strong' revisionist critics like Harold Bloom who can help us re-describe things, produce new narratives, new metaphors we can live by, and so forth. But then, if you look at Rorty's latest books, you find that he is still talking philosophy and, what's more, going back to the same technical issues – of truth, knowledge, representation, realism versus anti-realism – that pre-occupy his analytic colleagues, or ex-colleagues. He is still trying hard to get straight about those issues, to set other people straight and make sure that they haven't misunderstood him, yet at the same time he's denouncing that whole line of talk as hopelessly narrow and stifling. So, in a sense, you could say that the same thing's happening here; I mean, what have we been talking about today if not theory, its problems and prospects, the uses and abuses of theory? I suppose if you define theory more broadly, as a sort of intelligent, reflective self-consciousness about what we're doing when we do literary criticism, then the whole issue becomes less charged. Everyone wants to be that – they don't all want to be theorists, at least not to make 'theory' their academic specialism, but they do all want to be intelligent, reflective and self-critical about what they are doing.

Frank Kermode: But then you get the kind of meta-effect if you go up that route, the next layer of people being intelligent about people being intelligent about literature; and there has been a certain amount of that in the great efflorescence of theory in the last thirty years. People like myself – old-fashioned people who like texts (we can't even use that word now without bracketing it) – do get worried by the fact that, in our view (and maybe the view is incorrect, maybe there's been a kind of recursive effect), we're getting so far away from the study of literary artefacts, shall we say, that they're in danger of being totally neglected. That's my fear – I'm not afraid of theory, I'm afraid of meta-theory, and meta-meta-theory.

Michael Payne: Let me try my last question, and then maybe we'll have many more resourceful questions than this. Both of you have written a lot about music: Chris has a book on Shostakovich, and Frank Kermode reviews books on music – I recall several lengthy reviews which you wrote on Mozart, for example. Even professional musicologists describe how difficult it is to write about music, yet you have, both of you, crossed that disciplinary or artistic line. Was this simply because of some passion you have for music, or was it something that you wanted to say about music, that you found that musicologists were not saying?

Frank Kermode: Well, I like it, that's true; and I think, in certain curious ways, the analysis of a musical text is easier than the analysis of a poem. I mean that if you want to be very boring indeed, you can do quite elaborate musical analyses; I know Bernard Shaw, many years ago, said that if you applied the methods of music criticism to literature, you would analyse 'To be or not to be' in these terms: 'We commence with an infinitive, which is immediately inverted.' But I guess the answer to your question is simply that one likes it; you never have to write about anything you don't like, as long as you're off your own beat, you know. That would explain it for me – Chris will have a more profound explanation.

Christopher Norris: Well, I started to write about music because I lost interest in my PhD at a certain point; I had to earn some money so took up music journalism. Then I edited a couple of books – one on Shostakovich, the other called *Music and the Politics of Culture* – which I suppose you could describe as 'interventions', especially the Shostakovich book, which came out strongly against the predominant Western Cold-War 'revisionist' line on Shostakovich, the idea that his music is a constant running satire or attack on the Soviet system, and the fiercer the attack, the better the music. This struck me – strikes me still – as just a crude inversion of the standard Soviet line, the view of Shostakovich as a good 'socialist realist' at heart, although one who suffered occasional 'bourgeois-decadent' lapses from grace. Also I think it produces some very bad performances when conductors pick up on this revisionist line and go out of their way to make his music – especially his symphonic finales – sound as grim and humourless as possible.

Since then I've carried on writing about music, mainly about issues in music theory, aesthetics and the philosophy of music. In fact we have an MA course in Cardiff called 'Music and Cultural Politics' which really came out of that other book I edited, and which is jointly taught by people in the Music, History and Philosophy Departments. It has a lot to do with the way that new ideas from literary and cultural theory are migrating into musicology, the so-called 'New Musicology'. But I do have doubts about some of this stuff, especially the nowadays routine attack on notions of the musical 'canon', or the flat rejection of any idea that some works are better than others. This goes along with a similar attack on all those evaluative criteria – notions of unity, 'organic form', thematic transformation, long-range tonal development, etc. – which are likewise regarded, by the New Musicologists, as so many ideological constructs with highly conservative (not to say totalitarian) implications. And musical analysis also comes in for a lot of stick from these quarters since it is thought of as just a set of techniques for holding the canon in place, that is to say, for showing how the 'great works' of Western musical tradition are those that most strikingly exemplify the same set of values.

The most influential essay here was a piece by Joseph Kerman entitled 'How We Got Into Analysis, and How to Get Out', which appeared in the journal *Critical Inquiry* during the early 1980s. Since then it has become standard form, at least among the more theoretically inclined younger musicologists, to denounce 'organic form' and suchlike notions as remnants of an old-style 'aesthetic ideology' with some very nasty things behind it. Derrida has had some influence here, though often (I suspect) at second-hand, and there are also lots of references to Paul de Man, who of course devoted a main part of his later work to deconstructing organicist metaphors and pointing out their dangerous complicity with forms of 'national-aestheticist' thinking. So analysis has got itself a bad name among the new theorists although not so much among those who think – as I do – that you can not only learn a lot 'about' music but come to understand and enjoy it more profoundly by reading a piece of sharp-eared, perceptive, intelligent musical analysis.

Certainly there are some *kinds* of analysis – especially the kind developed by Heinrich Schenker – that do have this in-built bias toward music in the mainly Austro-German and 'high' classical-romantic line of descent. Also Schenker had some pretty repugnant political views and you can see how these views – along with his ana-lytic method – resulted in his low opinion (indeed, at times, his contemptuous dismissal) of music like Debus-sy's that didn't fit in with his preconceived ideas about organic form, thematic development and so forth. But this is not to say that *all* analysis amounts to just a kind of disguised apologetics for the ideological status quo, or something more sinister than that. Nor is it to say, as students often do, that notions like 'organic form' are just *post hoc* inventions or projections on the part of present-day analysts.

This is a fallacious argument, I think, like the idea put around by some cultural theorists that since the word 'literature' was used until about 1800 to cover all sorts of writing, and not just certain kinds of highly valued 'literary' text, therefore 'literature' didn't exist until the concept was invented in response to various ideological interests. I expect there is a label for this sort of fallacy but it escapes my mind at the moment. Anyway it is even more obvious in the case of music. The problem with 'literature' is that you can't easily say just which texts merit that title since some were once read (say) as historical, or scientific, or philosophical works but were then overtaken by the progress of scholarship, or by changes in scientific understanding, and are now read chiefly for their stylistic or narrative qualities. (Hume's historical writings would again be a good case in point.) And conversely, some works of fiction or poetry have lost their 'literary' appeal and are now read chiefly as historical source-texts, or as sociological documents.

So there's a special kind of problem about defining 'literature' which has to do with its elusiveness as a descriptive category. But it is not so hard for analysts to show that Haydn and Mozart were composing sonata-form movements – and composing works with a high degree of thematic and tonal integration – long before the music theorists came along and codified the forms in question. Of course the New Musicologists would say: well, there you go again, invoking those same old organicist values, and appealing to 'analysis' as if it had to do with something objectively *there* in the music, something that wasn't just a product of ideological or socio-political interests. Well, here I part company with the New Musicologists, since I think (and here I am speaking from personal experience) that analysis can tell us quite a lot about music, about why certain works, or certain passages of works, affect us as they do, why their impact is so powerful, why they have this otherwise inexplicable power to engage our responses at the deepest level. I suppose that what this really comes down to is a growing conviction that music is just too important – too much a part of the life worth living – to be theorized away in social, cultural or ideological terms.

This question comes up in the philosophy of mind where you get people like Jerry Fodor arguing that some mental functions (such as language) are relatively 'encapsulated', or 'cognitively impervious', by which they mean that, say, talking straight ahead and getting the grammar right is something that proceeds in virtual isolation from all the other things going on in our minds at any given time. This is a basically modular approach to cognitive pyschology that distinguishes specialized functions like these from other, more permeable functions that are not so localized in the brain and which draw on a whole variety of inputs, for instance, those of social context, or adaptive behavioural responses, or whatever we have learned in the way of theoretical knowledge. There is an interesting question here about music, that is, whether reading an analysis of this or that musical work can actually have some decisive effect on our *experience* of the work in question, rather than our 'knowledge' of it in some merely abstract, musicological sense. I think that it can, that musical understanding ('appreciation', if you like) can be greatly enhanced by this kind of analysis.

Of course the same applies to fields like linguistics where there is no point in offering a transformational-generative theory of the 'deep structure' underlying some surface ambiguity unless it can be checked against the knowledge of competent native speakers. This reminds me (again) of a point that Empson made in the closing chapter of *Seven Types of Ambiguity* – namely, that verbal analyses are all very well, and can turn up some wonderful things, but they are not going to convince anyone unless they work by making you more consciously aware of whatever it was that made the lines so haunting or memorable in the first place. Anyway I agree with Frank that if 'theory' is to earn its musicological keep then it had better connect with our musical responses and not set out from the negative ('deconstructive') premise that this is all just a product of our ideological conditioning. I feel very strongly about this and it has produced some heated, though I hope productive and rewarding, debates with my cultural-materialist colleagues on the MA course.

QUESTIONS FROM THE FLOOR

Gary Day: Chris, what was the perceived inadequacy of reading literature which made you move over into philosophy?

Christopher Norris: It wasn't so much that I just lost interest in literary criticism, or literary theory, it was more the way things were going in certain quarters, with the advent of a new 'theoretical' (mainly post-structuralist) orthodoxy. And I suppose there was a feeling in some of those quarters that Norris had flipped his lid, going on about truth, sticking up for 'Enlightenment' values, attacking the bogeyman of cultural relativism, and so forth. Also I was beginning to feel that had Philosophy been available at sixth-form level, or as an A-level subject, then I would have done Philosophy and most likely been happier, more at home in the field. Still, I have carried on reading fiction and poetry, and enjoying them, and on the other hand 'doing' philosophy, writing it and teaching it, which I now feel is not entirely separate from my old literary-critical interests.

Frank Kermode: You can't have thought that it was a very big jump that you took?

Christopher Norris: No; in fact, what got me interested in philosophy was partly your seminar and partly reading Empson. I came to feel that Empson was a marvellously gifted literary critic and had been recognized for that, but what I saw as his more philosophical work hadn't been anything like so widely recognized. It seemed worth banging the drum for Empson as a really important and original thinker about issues in philosophy of language.

Frank Kermode: Well, I am always for that.

John Schad: A question about religion, if I may. You could say there is an ironic twist in the respective careers, or histories, of Frank Kermode and Jacques Derrida. For Frank *used to* write about religion – not only, for example, in *The Genesis of Secrecy* but in his introduction to *The Tempest* where he writes of art as a 'means of Grace' (with a capital 'G') – but now, as Frank said last night, he has no interest in biblical criticism; in contrast, when Derrida first emerged he was perceived as a radically secular thinker whereas now completely the reverse – deconstruction's 'turn to religion' is almost a cliché. This is, perhaps, especially ironic given the conventional argument, as expressed by such as Jonathan Culler, that traditionally Anglo-American literary criticism is in some ways bound to Christianity (witness, of course, the New Critics). Again in contrast, we have been accustomed to think of philosophy, in particular French philosophy, as a necessarily secular enterprise.

Frank Kermode: Well, the first thing you make me want to say is that none of the work which you referred to, which was mostly done in the 1980s, on Biblical subjects, was religious – my books are totally without religion. If they weren't they would be, I'm afraid, very deceptive, because I'm not religious. Now, my interest was in biblical criticism which is, after all, older and in some ways more mature than literary criticism. I don't want to be autobiographical about this, but this interest began when I decided that I needed to read the gospels in Greek, which I did, and when I did that I saw immense puzzles, problems of all sorts, of a literary kind – not a religious kind at all. And then I read some of the great tradition of biblical commentary, which is, of course, primarily German, and I was astonished by the critical achievement of these people, of which I'd been totally ignorant; I knew a little bit about Strauss, and so on, but not much. And so I went to courses in this, and joined the Cambridge New Testament seminar, which was a very disappointing affair, I thought; so, when in the late 1970s, I was asked to give some lectures at Harvard, it was biblical criticism that was in my head – so that's how *The Genesis of Secrecy* happened. And that's had some sequels; but I think it partly spoils the irony you speak of that in fact they're not religious works at all; never intended to be – should not be taken as such.

Michael Payne: I think, Frank, that perhaps pertinent here is a review that you wrote of paintings of Jesus, in which I think you said something like: 'it's important to recall that the original viewers of these paintings were in a very different relationship to the subject matter, than most contemporary viewers'. Am I recalling that correctly?

Frank Kermode: I think this must have been the big exhibition at the National Gallery a couple of years ago.[1]

Michael Payne: Yes, which perhaps ties up with something that you have been saying earlier this morning about the conferral of value by the reader of a text, or a viewer of a painting. Did you not speak about that? I keep badgering you about the question: where does the value come from?

Frank Kermode: Well, this is a big topic. That exhibition, which was a very good one, was run by Neil MacGregor at the National Gallery, who's a Catholic. Of course, like a good entrepreneur, he wanted to make the exhibition equally relevant to people of all faiths, which is a non-starter. When I wrote that piece this is the thing that was worrying me, that he had not actually succeeded. There was also a television series attached to the exhibition, which he ran with an increasing note of Catholic piety, I thought, all of which I deplored. So what I was thinking about was, how difficult it is to stage an exhibition of that sort in such a way that it's absolutely denominationally neutral, as you might say. This, I guess, has got something to do with the question which you put.

The other one could last us for the rest of the day, because it really does raise problems of hermeneutics, which we haven't really been bothering much about, as far as I can make out – the so-called fusion of horizons, and all the rest of it. My view is that nobody will have any true contact with a work of art if it isn't modern; I mean that if it isn't modern then it has to be made so, and it's made so largely by commentary. What keeps things alive, as I've been saying, is what people say about them, and informed commentary is really something which makes works accessible and relevant which otherwise are very, very remote from our cultural set-up. You may want to say that such commentary is a false addition to some original artefact, but I wouldn't agree – how else would it survive? How else do we have the possibility of a genuine encounter with a Raphael, or a Botticelli? This connects, of course, with why these things drop out; people stop attending to them and they die. Sometimes they don't quite die, and then they're revived, as in the case of Botticelli, for example. It's quite a common story in the history of painting: things that are greatly admired, then cease to be admired, and then are restored for quite other reasons; for instance, people like Swinburne and Pater restored Botticelli not because they were deeply intimate with the Florence of the 1490s, but because they rather fancied this kind of girl, or some such reason. I mean, there are all sorts of reasons for either prolonging or reviving informed interest in works of art that would have otherwise slipped out of attention; and I think in that sense modernity is something we can add pretty well to anything – we can try to, and sometimes we succeed.

Michael Payne: Maybe we can end with the other side of John's question about religion; namely, the Talmudic side of Derrida's thought and his work – Chris, you've written a little bit about that.

Christopher Norris: Yes, but I'm not the best person to ask; I'm no Talmudic scholar, and besides, this whole revival of religious or theological interests among literary theorists is something that I find pretty hard to take. When people are killing each other all over the world in the name of this or that half-baked fanatical religious creed it is the last thing we need to have literary intellectuals egging them on from the sidelines. I expect it was reading Bertrand Russell's *Why I Am Not a Christian* – at an impressionable age, no doubt – that cured me of religion once and for all. Also, much later, there was reading Hume, whom I always recommend to religiously inclined students as an antidote to some of the ideas they have picked up on other courses. And then of course Empson spent a lot of time, in his later years, attacking what he saw as the morally corrosive influence of the 'neo-Christian' revival in literary criticism, a movement that he thought had done great harm to critics' powers of evaluative judgement. I think he would have been even more shocked by the way things are going nowadays among various theorists with a new-found taste for Levinasian talk about the ethics of deconstruction conceived as a quasi-theological discourse of radical alterity, absolute 'otherness', and so forth. I want to say that this is a highly undesirable, as well as philosophically confused, way of thinking, especially at a time when so many barbarous acts are condoned in the name of this or that revived fundamentalist creed.

One of Derrida's earliest essays, first published in 1964, was a long and detailed critique of Levinas which seems to me spot-on in explaining what is wrong with this idea of radical alterity, or respect for the infinite other.[2] The trouble is that it all too easily flips over into thinking of other people as so utterly different from us that they no longer have a claim on our sense of shared humanity. More recently, of course, Derrida has written much more sympathetically about Levinas, and has taken to talking about ethical decisions – the dizzying moment of ethical choice – in terms of this encounter with an absolute otherness that breaks with all existing moral codes,

conventions, decision procedures, principled justifica-
tions, etc. In this case, he says, a choice of action is
'ethical' only on condition that it can't be justified, that
it involves a kind of Kierkegaardian leap of faith, a
decision to suspend all the values that normally count as
ethically or humanly binding.

I mentioned a moment ago that Derrida has a lot in
common with Kierkegaard; yet when Derrida finally gets
around to writing about Kierkegaard at some length
which text does he choose but *Fear and Trembling*, that
hideous 'vindication' of religious faith as a willingness,
on Abraham's part, to sacrifice his son Isaac at God's
mysterious (no doubt infinitely 'other') behest. It seems
to me that this whole emphasis on radical alterity and
this idea of genuine, authentic ethical choice as a leap
into the supra-human beyond had better be taken with
a large pinch of salt if we want to preserve any sense of
shared humanity across various cultural, ideological or
religious differences. Of course it will be said that I am
merely displaying my attachment to quaint old humanist
conceptions of ethical community and value. Well, I
have to plead guilty to that, although I don't think the
charge holds up if you really think through the alter-
natives on offer.

So yes, the recent 'religious' turn in Derrida's writing
that you were talking about is in striking contrast with
his early work. He used to go out of his way to insist that
he wasn't some sort of latter-day Meister Eckhart
defining the attributes of God in negative terms, or in
terms of what lay outside and beyond the utmost
powers of human comprehension. In fact there is a

splendid passage in one of Derrida's early books, *Speech and Phenomena*, where he lists about a half-dozen reasons why deconstruction is *not* any kind of negative theology, or gesture toward some transcendent, paradoxical truth beyond the limits of mere human reason. But he seems to have softened his line on that, partly I suppose through the *rapprochement* with Levinas, and partly – perhaps – through exposure to the strain of postmodern 'atheological' thinking promoted by people like Mark C. Taylor who have moved on from the kinds of position adopted by death-of-God theologians such as Thomas Altizer in the late 1960s. So he often tends to say, when questioned on this, that 'deconstruction' is not his to dispose of, or to lay down rules for its correct application. It has grafted itself into other contexts, including various kinds of religious discourse, and what right has he to protest 'they've got me wrong'? Of course it is good to be tolerant of other viewpoints but I do sometimes wish that Derrida would take a stronger line on what other people have made of his work.

Frank Kermode: I remember he was very sensitive about the negative theology charge, wasn't he? Is 'apophatic' another name for the same thing? It is, isn't it? It's also a rhetorical term – it means pretending in a speech that you don't know what you're going to say next, which Derrida does a lot of; that's one of his great tricks. So he is apophatic, in one sense, but not in another, and this was the point he made in a discussion that I heard once in Jerusalem; I thought that meant he was rather attracted, really, by the idea of negative theology. He had that curious idea from Plato's *Timaeus*, which I think Kristeva also has, of the *chora*; he used that in a rather mystical way too, he was being pretty mystical that day.

Michael Payne: Well, perhaps the next time we have one of these conversations we might pick up on this rhetorical trope you're speaking about, and ask whether a man who titles his autobiography *Not Entitled* might actually have been writing under this trope for a very long time. Thank you, Frank, and thank you, Chris.

5

feminist theory after theory
Toril Moi

BIOGRAPHICAL NOTE ─────

Toril Moi is currently Professor of Literature and Romance Studies at Duke University in the USA. Her interest in theory began, however, in her native Norway where she completed a PhD in Comparative Literature before moving to Oxford, England in the early eighties. Here she was one among a number of young critics whose interest in theory was closely allied to left-wing political commitment, a combination that, as Moi herself discovered, did not always make for employability in Thatcherite Britain, or at least not in Oxford. The situation did not necessarily improve when, in 1985 Moi, published *Sexual/Textual Politics,* her landmark study of feminist theory from the literary criticism of Kate Millet and Mary Ellmann to the poststructural theorizing of Hélène Cixous, Luce Irigaray and Julia Kristeva. Though her discussion of the last was in many ways critical, Moi for a while became identified with poststructuralist feminism and its anti-essentialist account of a fluid, unfixed and decentred subjectivity. This identification grew as she went on to edit *The Kristeva Reader* in 1986; indeed, Moi acknowledged a particular identification with Kristeva who, as a Bulgarian in Paris, knew what it meant to think and write as a foreign woman, or *étrangère*.

In the nineties, however, Moi became increasingly asso-ciated with the life and work of an earlier Parisian figure, namely Simone de Beauvoir – in 1990 Moi published *Feminist Theory and Simone de Beauvoir* and then in 1994 she wrote *Simone de Beauvoir: The Making of an Intellectual Woman*. Moi's interest in Beauvoir's 'feminism of freedom', an exis-tential feminism, also led her to draw increasingly on such 'ordinary language' philosophers as Ludwig Wittgenstein, J. L. Austin and Stanley Cavell. These influences are well to the fore in 1999 when, exactly fifty years after the publication of Beauvoir's *The Second Sex*, Moi published her most recent and much-celebrated book, *What is a Woman?* (1999), the title of which echoes such famous philosophical questions as Imma-nuel Kant's 'What is Enlightenment?' and Jean-Paul Sartre's *What is Literature?* Moi wants the question of women and feminism to gain 'access to the universal', which means that they should be part of any political, social, cultural or intel-lectual practice. This again leads Moi to Beauvoir in whom Moi sees not only a feminist but a philosopher, and in parti-cular a philosopher who offers an embodied, 'everyday' account of the human subject; an account that in many ways has parallels to the account of subjectivity that Moi finds in the work of French sociologist Pierre Bourdieu. In the inter-view that follows, Moi's attention to woman as an embodied human subject leads to an engagement with the universal declaration of human rights. To think through these rights in concrete, everyday terms is, she argues, part of the public responsibility of the intellectual. One might just say that, for Moi, this is life after theory.

Michael Payne : I would like to begin by asking you what has changed since *Sexual/Textual Politics* was published back in 1985.

Toril Moi : Women now find themselves as marginalized as they ever were in theory-related contexts. I mean more marginalized than in 1985. Lots of big theoretical debates carry on – about meaning and modernity, globalism, postmodernity and so on – and people make their contributions, give their lectures and write their papers, and they'll be very theoretically sophisticated, *but* there won't be a word about either feminism or women in them. Back in 1985 the whole point of having feminist theory was that concerns that had to do with women were supposed to be as important as all other concerns in every theoretical context. No psychoanalysis or deconstruction or Foucault-inspired theory without women, as it were. Well, no longer so, apparently. It annoys me also that it's only women who keep mentioning this sorry state of affairs. Just as I can discuss modernity with him, a male theorist – Perry Anderson, say – could discuss women's and feminism's place in modernity with me, right? Well, it's just not happening.

Michael Payne: There's that wonderful passage in *Three Guineas* where Virginia Woolf envisions a time when men and women are working together for the same cause; but as you say, that's not happened.

Toril Moi: Well, the point is rather that when men and women do work together for the same cause, then the cause is still likely to reflect the men's interest. Of late I have returned to Simone de Beauvoir's formulation, and now want to say that what is going on here is that *women are denied access to the universal*. 'Universal' here just means the general category, not something deeply metaphysical. So, for example, if we are talking about the category *theory*, women should have access to it without having to pretend that they're not women (by going along with men's interests, by excluding their own sexed and gendered subjectivity). This, in part, is what I write about in Essay II in *What is a Woman?*, where I discuss what I call 'Simone de Beauvoir's dilemma'. This shows how a sexist society offers women two equally unacceptable options: either we can masquerade as abstract individuals or we can be imprisoned in a fantasmatic notion of femininity. Beauvoir speaks of the 'choice' between having to *eliminate* one's sexed subjectivity and being *imprisoned* in it. Both options are traps for women. So, feminist theory has to reject both options, and also show that they are at work in all kinds of situations, including theoretical situations, today. Women need access to the universal as women. Otherwise we'll never get anything that will approach genuine equality between the sexes. I'm getting more distressed about this because it seems to me that the production of theory is carrying on as before, that feminism has been ghettoized as 'oh, that's what some women do. Men don't need to worry about all that.' This is unfortunate.

Michael Payne: It was with the hope of addressing this question, of course, that we wanted you to be a part of this volume, and to have your voice heard.

Toril Moi: I know that. I could, of course, say that this is precisely to ghettoize the question of women, yet again. I become the token woman who is supposed to guarantee the political correctness of the context. This allows the participating men to carry on talking about men under the label of 'theory', as before. This produces the impression that *theory* is what men do; *feminist* theory is what women do. Yet I think it is better to participate and say what I think than not. So far, at least. There was a moment in the early 1980s (do you remember?), it was a flourishing theory moment when there were lots of conferences, and all sorts of feminists – Freudian, Foucaldian, postmodernist, deconstructionist – were all at the same conferences. I think the last high point of that might have been the 'Sexuality' conference at Southampton. I forget what year it was in, perhaps 1986? But some time in the late 1980s we all became specialists on separate theories, which inevitably meant that men no longer bothered to pretend that feminist thought was relevant to them.

Michael Payne: I had the impression, though, that during those years theory was being pursued on the two sides of the Atlantic almost from opposite or opposing intellectual classes, in the sense that it was the aristocratic universities in the States – Yale, Duke, California

Irvine, Cornell and so on – that were the big theory producers, in contrast to the grass-roots activity that was taking place at the new and red-brick universities in Britain. So it seemed to me that there was much more of a continuation of radical politics in theory production in England than in the States.

Toril Moi: I think that's probably true. I began my work on theory in Norway – that's where I was trained; I came to England just after finishing my PhD. It seems to me that the whole point back then was the *politics* of theory. At that time I was living in Oxford, I was a member of a group of people in the early 1980s who were either unemployed or just finishing their education. The whole point then was that theory was seen as a way to attack 'the powers that be'. It was intellectual dynamite. At that time the people in Oxford who were considered 'the powers that be' were doing philology or empiricist biography or something. That's what *we* thought, anyway.

I applied for a job in Oxford just after S*exual/Textual Politics* came out, and I was interviewed by a committee of twenty men, or something like that. The very first question was 'Now, Dr Moi, you clearly want to destroy this institution, so why are you applying for a position with us?' It's true! And you know, at one level I was annoyed, but at another level it supported the belief that theory, just by virtue of being theory, was radical. To be precise: I don't believe that theory is intrinsically political. I didn't then, and I don't now. Theory qua theory is not necessarily political or political in any special way. Like all other human activities it always has to be understood in the relation to its concrete historical and social situation. But in that social situation, theory was certainly radical. Obviously, I didn't get the job, but I had the feeling that what I wrote really mattered to people. That it even made some people feel a little frightened. That was quite reassuring to me.

Michael Payne: Maybe we can move back a little bit here, not to move away from this question, but perhaps to approach it in a slightly different way. In rereading the preface to part two of *What is a Woman?*, I was really struck by how openly self-reflective you are there, first of all about the reviews and critical responses to *Sexual/Textual Politics*, and also about the direction that your own work has taken since that book came out. I'm going to offer you a characterization of that direction and ask you to reject this or correct it in any way that you'd like. One way to think about it is that you have, in a sense, moved from a concentration on Julia Kristeva to a concentration on Simone de Beauvoir, and also from a theoretical emphasis that involves a certain critical, but nevertheless genuine, appropriation of Derrida and Lacan and Foucault to an emphasis on Bourdieu and 'ordinary language' philosophy, particularly Wittgenstein, J. L. Austin and Stanley Cavell. Is that the way it's gone?

Toril Moi: Yes, I think that's right. But if you tell the story that way it sounds like a conversion. I would like to stress that right from the start I was always reading Beauvoir and I was always reading Freud, even when I was also reading French theory and Lacan. Beauvoir has always been with me. I first read *The Second Sex* in Norwegian when I was fifteen. If you look carefully at *Sexual/ Textual Politics*, you will see that most of it is perfectly compatible with Beauvoirean feminism. Beauvoir was an anti-essentialist, so was I. Fundamentally, I thought essentialism was bad because one should not produce unwarranted generalizations about women. I didn't really care that deeply about the 'metaphysics' of it. So when I am critical of Irigaray, for example, in *Sexual/ Textual Politics*, what drove me was my outrage at the way in which she presented women as babbling, inco- herent creatures. While some women may well be like that, most of us are not. So, the sense of continuity in my work is based on Beauvoir, Freud and a lifelong com- mitment to feminism. In fact, I'm working on a feminist and psychoanalytical paper, on femininity, right now, it's a critique of some central Lacanian concepts, from a feminist and Wittgenstein-inspired point of view.

Michael Payne: The two readers you edited, the *Kristeva Reader* and *French Feminist Thought* both came out at about the same time. I guess they're about a year apart.

Toril Moi: Yes, the *Kristeva Reader* 1986, and the other one 1987.

Michael Payne: And, of course, in *French Feminist Thought* Beauvoir has pride of place; she is there right at the beginning. So, anyone who thinks of you as starting with Kristeva and then moving to Beauvoir would be wrong, I guess.

Toril Moi: One thing you have to notice is the cover of the *Kristeva Reader*, the Piero della Francesca painting called *The Nativity.* There is a nice intertextual relationship to Beauvoir there too. If you look in the index of the book, there are only one or two references to Beauvoir. But the one time Kristeva comments on Beauvoir is when she criticizes Beauvoir's claim that this painting is an example of sexism, because the Virgin is kneeling in adoration before her male offspring. Kristeva takes issue with that. I picked the painting for the cover because I saw it as a meeting place for two very powerful intellectual women. And of course, it is very beautiful.

Michael Payne: So, what we're doing now, is correcting the simplistic story that I was talking about, a linear account of a movement from Kristeva to Beauvoir? Is there, then, no sense in which what you've been doing is recovering what life was like *before* theory?

Toril Moi: Intellectually speaking, I'm probably too young to have had a life before theory. I was barely in my teens, living in a small Norwegian village, when the students took to the barricades in Paris. At the time I didn't know a word of French, and had no sense at all of what was happening there. My specific generation, we who were born roughly from 1951 to 1959, are *belated* in relation to the movement you call 'theory'. I certainly have always felt that. Which means that I have always had a complicated relationship to it.

If you look at what is still with me from post-structuralism, what I really responded to, it's all the poststructuralist theories that are compatible with interesting versions of psychoanalysis. Ideas about the decentred subject, about human beings as always embodied, always libidinal. This, of course, is very similar to Beauvoir and Merleau-Ponty's understanding of human beings as embodied situations. (I write about this in the title essay of *What is a Woman*? and also in an essay called 'Is Anatomy Destiny', included in the same collection, where I discuss Freud's view of the body.) I imagine there are three positions you can take on the subject these days: one is that any articulation of sub-jectivity is metaphysical. Another is to say, 'Well, let's get back to the traditional, full, liberal, human subject', though I don't think there are really many people who believe in that. These two options often get caught in a 'see-saw' or mirror-image relationship to each other. In my view, there is a third position, which is the idea of the decentred subject. This is a subject that acts, that has responsibility and that certainly exists. But it is also fra-gile, unstable, the product of its situation and in cease-less interchange with that situation, which has to be understood as the body, as well as history, social struc-tures, politics and so on. I suppose this is a slightly more fragile version of what has been called the subject of praxis. All the theorists I like reading have some version of this.

Michael Payne: I was intending, given the way in which you go back and critically reflect on your past work, to ask questions like: What aspects of *Sexual/Textual Politics* do you still wish to confirm? What do you see there that was important in the boldness and directness of the argument? What other things do you wish to correct? What you tend to do reminds me, in fact, of how Freud kept reading himself.

Toril Moi: Well, there's a danger in doing that too much because it may sound incredibly self-indulgent. I did write a brief retrospective piece as part of the introduction to *What is a Woman?* because I needed to situate the *new* work. I'm not generally too keen on going over my past work in public. Why not get on with it and say something new and exciting? Yet people do ask me questions about previous work. It is very hard to get the balance right between saying things that are helpful and illuminating to someone, and just endlessly staring at one's own navel.

Michael Payne: Well, I didn't read it that way, at all. I suppose I am referring to only a few pages in *What is a Woman?* – some in the preface and some in the introduction to part two. My point is that to turn intellectual work, at certain critical points, into a first-person narrative is a very important thing to do because it *situates* that work, it announces the critical reflectiveness of the person whom you're reading.

Toril Moi: Yes, one of the things that I have developed the most in my recent work is what it means to speak of *the personal*. This interest surely has its roots in a fascination with theories of the speaking subject. My early interest in Kristeva was, first of all, based on total admiration for a very brilliant woman who managed to get on in a very male-dominated field. But secondly, her key term, way back then, was always *the speaking subject*. That's what the first essay in *The Kristeva Reader* – 'The System and the Speaking Subject' – is all about. It is a sense of embodiment which you also get in Freud, Merleau-Ponty and Beauvoir.

Michael Payne: That essay was also a tremendously important opening of her work to an English-speaking audience. I believe it appeared in the *Times Literary Supplement* in English, back in 1973.

Toril Moi: Yes, it was, I suppose, her arrival on the English scene.

Michael Payne: Now I'd like to move along to one other thing, and that is the subtitle of your book on Beauvoir which is, of course, *Simone de Beauvoir: The Making of an Intellectual Woman*. You often use such words as 'intellectual', 'philosophical', 'theoretical' and, I wonder, are you using those words interchangeably? Not just in that book, but also in *What is a Woman?*

Toril Moi: It all depends on the context. In some situations they are interchangeable, in others not. In chapter two of *What is a Woman?*, I stage a discussion between many different kinds of thinkers. Some are philosophers, some call themselves theorists. In that context, either will do. But this is possible now. In the first half of the 1980s, 'theory' as a category just didn't exist. *Sexual/ Textual Politics* has a subtitle: *Feminist **Literary** Theory.* I certainly thought I was doing *literary* theory, not just 'theory' back then. I write about the shift of the meaning of theory in the new afterword to the second edition of *Sexual/Textual Politics*, which has just appeared. Nowadays, I suppose, 'theory' means something like poststructuralist theories of language and meaning, and certain kinds of feminist and Marxist schools of thought.

Michael Payne: My question arises in part from a passage in Wittgenstein's *Philosophical Investigations* where he introduces his discussion about what philosophy is, and what it does. There he starts it out with a rejection of theory. He says, 'One may not advance any kind of theory.'

Toril Moi: Yes, exactly. Wittgenstein is not, of course, using 'theory' there in the recent sense that I just outlined. For me, one of the attractive things about Wittgenstein is that he helps to disperse the fog that keeps our thoughts woolly, and our concepts unclear. His famous claim that 'philosophy leaves everything as it is' has nothing to do with political conservatism, as some people have said. Wittgenstein uses the word 'philosophy' negatively. For him it usually means metaphysics, language that's on holiday, language that runs on empty, like an engine that's idling – that's the image he uses. And, of course, I happen to think that an awful lot of theory – particularly in the last ten years – has been language that's idling. I don't think that it matters very much what we call our thinking, as long as we are clear about what we mean. Philosophers often have a kind of a priori idea about the nature of philosophy, and then spend their lives policing the boundaries of philosophy. That's a very negative outlook on thought! One of the results of that is of course that Simone de Beauvoir is excluded from philosophy. It's better to spend time with thought that *isn't* idling, that speaks to our most central concerns.

Michael Payne: This has to do with your using the word 'intellectual', say, rather than the word 'philosophical'?

Toril Moi: When I use the word 'intellectual' it's partly – in the case of Sartre and Beauvoir – because that was what they called themselves; they lived at a time in France when that was the term. However, I also use the word because I think it indicates someone who is trying not to be just a narrow specialist in a discipline. When the theory wave began, people who came to theory were trying to be intellectuals. To do theory was, initi- ally, something you did over and in addition to some other specialty that you might have. You couldn't *just* be a theorist, and you certainly couldn't train in 'theory' anywhere. The early days were inspiring because people came to theory from all sorts of different backgrounds and were more broad in their training. Now, on the other hand, we are training a whole generation of scholars who are simply theorists. Sometimes I worry that they won't have anything but theory to talk about. Talk about the danger of producing empty language!

Michael Payne: I wonder if you would agree that 'intellectual' also suggests more of a breaking into a public sphere, whereas 'theoretical' or 'philosophical' might not imply that at all.

Toril Moi: These days people wonder why there are no longer any public intellectuals. On the other hand they also complain that intellectuals who do speak to the media, are prostituting themselves, given the power of the media these days. It certainly would be very difficult to be a genuine public intellectual today. In the US, some African–American scholars are considered an example of the category, but nobody has the kind of stature and impact that Sartre and Beauvoir used to have in mid-twentieth-century France.

Michael Payne: I'd like to take you back to Kristeva for a just a minute. It seems to me that Kristeva's position as an outsider was very important to you. There's a wonderful moment in *Sexual/Textual Politics* where you break out into the first person yourself and say that you really felt an identification with her as an outsider.

Toril Moi: Well, she came from one language and started working in another. That's obviously a point of identification for me. I think she made that into her greatest intellectual strength.

Michael Payne: There's a critical advantage there, is there not?

Toril Moi: Yes, if you use it right, because being on the margin you can get a vantage point that makes you see something that people who are more centrally placed don't see. Of course, if you see those things and become very successful as a result, then you aren't on the margins anymore. There's no essential marginality.

Michael Payne: The other thing I particularly noticed was your appropriation of her genealogical sense of women's time, which you, in a sense, incorporated into the argument of *Sexual/Textual Politics*. And I wonder whether the Kristevan sense of women's time still seems important to you?

Toril Moi: Kristeva's very influential essay 'Women's Time' was based on an analysis of the stages of feminism that most people shared at the time. The idea was that the first feminists, the suffragettes, wanted *equality.* This is normally interpreted as women wanting to be like men. Then the revolt of the 1960s and 1970s led to an emphasis on *difference.* Finally, and this was Kristeva's contribution, we were going to have to get *beyond difference* by becoming radically anti-essentialist, and deconstructing the opposition between equality and difference. I think I really liked Kristeva's analysis because it gave me a hope that we could think beyond that sterile opposition between equality and difference. The problem, I now realize, is that the analysis is based on that opposition. A book like Joan Scott's *Only Para-doxes to Offer* is an important example of recent work based on the same opposition. Like Kristeva, Scott also struggles to get beyond the terms of her own argument, only to conclude that all we can have is a paradoxical relationship to the goals of feminism.

I'm now inclined to think that the mistake is to posit that there is a fundamental opposition between equality and difference to start with. This is both a logical and a historical mistake. In the context we are talking about, the opposite of equality is not difference, but inequality. To speak of women wanting to be like men is beside the point here, for we are not talking about what human beings are like, but about social and political rights. And, historically, the suffragettes who wanted equal rights were deeply committed to differentialist theories of femininity. Even today, so-called difference-feminists aren't, in fact, in favour of inequality. The opposition doesn't work. We need to reformulate the whole thing. We need to look at this opposition; we need to change it, and we need to come up with another way of describing feminism.

Michael Payne: Do you think that the genealogical history of feminism as a movement – whether intellectual or historical – is recapitulated in the lives of individual women? I'm thinking, in part, of my own female students. Every year I see young women coming to feminist theory for the first time and it is almost as though they have to replicate the history of feminism in terms of their own growing awareness of things.

Toril Moi: Not really. The privileged undergraduates I see at Duke tend to think that they live in a perfect meritocracy. They don't feel discriminated against. Many won't until they try to get equal rights at work, or when they have to confront the challenges of going to work while bringing up small children. Men who go to work while bringing up small children usually do not have the same difficulties, curiously enough.

Michael Payne: And now, of course, women are in the numerical majority at colleges and universities.

Toril Moi: Yes, so to that kind of student you can't come and say, 'look you're so horribly oppressed'. That's not going to work.

Michael Payne: I was struck when rereading *What is a Woman?* that in your extraordinarily careful reading of the opening sections of *The Second Sex* you strongly emphasize Beauvoir's work as a philosopher, and especially as an existential philosopher. The post-structuralists, though, especially Lacan and Derrida, were very dismissive of existentialism.

Toril Moi: I know they were. Judith Butler is very interesting here, because she wrote about Beauvoir early on, and actually invokes both Beauvoir and Sartre in *Gender Trouble*. Indeed, you could say that half of Butler's theory of gender-as-performance is Sartre's 'we are what we do', the other half is a more or less Foucault-inspired 'there is no doer behind the deed'. Butler, though, *is* an exception; she has a much more interesting relationship to existentialism than other theorists that she is, otherwise, closer to.

I suppose I would say that when the poststructuralists criticized Sartre it had much to do with the fact that the influential figures were students in the 1950s. Since Sartre was the great father figure at that time, he obviously had to be toppled. To put it in Bourdieuean terms: he had all the symbolic capitals, and they were the new generation, the would-be inheritors. You have, though, a different story with the somewhat younger generation. Bernard-Henri Lévy published his book on Sartre (*Le siècle de Sartre*) in 2000, I think. He honestly admits something that I had always suspected – namely, that he had been mouthing off about Sartre in his early work without actually having read much if any Sartre at that time. He had just followed the lead of the older master-thinkers (who definitely did read Sartre). I suspect that this ignorance of Sartre was widespread among the generation who came of intellectual age in, let's say, around 1968 when Sartre was waning and the new hot thing was to read Derrida, Foucault, Lacan, etc. They would, therefore, be massively critical of Sartre but they wouldn't have really *read* Sartre. It's not only Sartre who gets caught up in this, it's Beauvoir too. (Interesting here is Frantz Fanon who was, of course, very much inspired by Sartrean phenomenology, particularly in *Black Skin, White Masks,* and yet some poststructuralist readings of Fanon have tried to pretend that he was a poststructuralist all along.)

However, the point I want to stress is that if you really read Sartre and Beauvoir you find that they are not at all saying a lot of the things that some poststructuralists claim that they are saying. Existentialism was after all in opposition to all sorts of metaphysical essentialism. The whole point was that *existence precedes essence,* which means that the individual constructs meanings through practices in human situations. The problem that some people have with Sartre and Beauvoir is the very idea that there *is* a subject. But for Sartre consciousness is what we are, and consciousness is strictly defined as nothing – nothingness. To be is to be nothing, is part of the paradoxical message of *Being and Nothingness.* In short, I don't think Sartre has been well read these last twenty years, except by experts of course.

Michael Payne: It's interesting you should suggest that existentialism has survived theory.

Toril Moi: Well, I think theory did in some sense put an end to existentialism. I started planning my book on Beauvoir straight after *Sexual/Textual Politics* – that was the late 1980s – and I was, at that time, the only theorist I knew working on Beauvoir. But now it's changing.

Michael Payne: Were you interested in the idea of joint authorship between Sartre and Beauvoir, for a while? I am thinking of the way you refer to the authorship of the 1947 *What Is Literature?* You say there, 'Well, call it by Sartre because that name is on the title page.' Several times you have made the point that there was a very close intellectual collaboration, that it's often mistakenly been said that Beauvoir was on the receiving end of

Sartre's influence, and that there has not been enough attention to the influence in the other direction.

Toril Moi: Yes, I do think that's true, and particularly with *What Is Literature?* since it's based on an article co-signed by everyone on the editorial board, and since it also in part draws on ideas Beauvoir had already expressed in print. But of course Beauvoir probably developed those ideas in conversation with Sartre, just as he developed the same ideas in the same conversations with her. My point is that nobody would automatically postulate a one-way relationship between two *male* intellectuals who discussed ideas every day. But when there is a man and a woman, and particularly if they are also known to be lovers, then it's automatic: *he* influenced her. It's all very tedious and predictable.

Michael Payne: Perhaps we could move on to your interest in Pierre Bourdieu. *What is a Woman?* includes, of course, two important synthesizing essays on his work; however, in the wake of Bourdieu's recent death, there have been several attempts to determine his legacy. May I ask what you see as the most important, or perhaps the most enduring, aspect of his legacy?

Toril Moi: I think of Bourdieu as belonging to that philosophical tradition that is interested in the particular and concrete manifestations of human behaviour, and that understands the subject to be a subject of praxis, as Charles Taylor calls it. I write about this in the short essay called 'The Challenge of the Particular Case', where I relate him to writers such as Freud, Wittgenstein, Merleau-Ponty and, of course, Beauvoir. I am also a rather unusual reader of Bourdieu because I emphasize the way he understands human subjectivity. Bourdieu's work helps us to see human beings as social agents, as the products of the interaction between *habitus* and *field*, in the struggle for symbolic capital.[1] I don't think we can do without a social theory of the subject, and Bourdieu offers a good one.

Michael Payne: I wonder whether the greater openness to Derrida than to Bourdieu has to do with the fact that Bourdieu was a sociologist, and that there is a divide here that people in the humanities have to overcome. It seems to be thought – I think particularly by people who teach literature – that sociology is one of the lowliest subjects of all.

Toril Moi: Yes, I do think that there's a hierarchy of disciplines. That's for sure. But I also think that Bourdieu's work only became available – or started to get noticed beyond his own field – well after the implantation of Derridean literary criticism. That took hold fairly early in America, as early as the 1970s, and Bourdieu wasn't really *widely* read until the 1990s. So, by that point, you already have a strong hierarchy of people established as champions of a different school of theory. At this stage they are not going to change. Bourdieu then became a marginal figure in relation to that hegemony in America. So, yes, I'm sure it has to do with discipline, but it also has to do with temporality.

Bourdieu just didn't make his really big contributions at the same early time as Derrida. *Distinction* was published in French in 1979, and came out in English in 1984, when deconstruction had already fought and won its major battles in the United States.

Secondly, of course – this is something I say in 'The Challenge of the Particular Case' – if you want something that you can do close readings with in literature classes (which is the handy thing about a certain kind of poststructuralism) then Bourdieu is useless. It's extremely difficult to do something like a methodologically sound Bourdieuean reading in a short time, because you need to go out and gather a lot of relevant information first. Even though Bourdieu and his colleagues had already investigated the relevant educational institutions, I found the Bourdieuean research I was doing for my book on Beauvoir to be hard work. And I just tried to understand what it meant to become a philosopher for a woman in France in the 1920s. I needed to learn a lot about the history and sociology of educational institutions in France for example. One could, I suppose, do semantic readings of Bourdieu, and find examples in novels of people grabbing for symbolic capital but that's not very interesting.

Michael Payne: Also, he did not negotiate his opening into the English language at the famous 'Critical Languages and Sciences of Man' conference in Baltimore, at Johns Hopkins.

Toril Moi: Quite; again I think it's timing. The Baltimore conference was 1966 – so, where was Bourdieu in 1966? He didn't publish *Outline of a Theory of Practice* until 1972, and back in 1966 he hadn't written much. He'd done some work in Algeria, and he'd done *Les héritiers* (*The Inheritors*), you know, the reproduction of intellectual capital among French students, and some other stuff. So timing was crucial here.

Michael Payne: And those early books had a specifically French audience, and a specific punch for that audience, wouldn't you say?

Toril Moi: That's true, some of that work can't be directly generalized in the way that Derridean theory can. But I do think that your theory about sociology versus literature and philosophy is also important. If you add to that a kind of *décalage* in time of almost twenty years, then you have a totally different situation. In this sense, when discussing their influence in the United States, Bourdieu and Derrida aren't directly comparable.

Michael Payne: But aren't they contemporaries, Bourdieu and Derrida?

Toril Moi: Oh, yes, in terms of their year of birth, both were born around 1930, I believe. I'm talking about when they start doing their important work, when they start getting read in America. This is what Germans call *ungleichzeitigkeit*, 'unsimultaneity', which means that two phenomena that literally occur at the same time aren't in fact theorizable as part of the same historical moment.

Michael Payne: Well, this next question is on the same kind of structural line, but it's focused slightly differently. You've done a lot of careful work to show that feminism is culturally contingent as a politics, and also as a theory – that what's important in French feminism and what's important in Anglo-American feminism may be quite different, not only at different historical moments, but even at same moment.

Toril Moi: Oh, yes. I do believe that.

Michael Payne: Okay. So, with that background, taking this temporal and geographical contingency into account . . .

Toril Moi: Can we call it 'specificity' rather than pure 'contingency'?

Michael Payne: Sure, let's call it specificity; so, with *that* in mind, would you be willing to say what you think the most pressing concerns in feminism are now?

Toril Moi: The situation for women is, of course, not quite the same as the situation of feminist theorists. So is the question, 'What's the most important thing for women?' or is the question 'What's most important for feminist theory?'

Michael Payne: I see the difference. Let it be whichever one you wish to speak about.

Toril Moi: Right. Well, first of all you need to distinguish between women in very developed societies and those elsewhere. In Western societies women achieved abstract equal rights in the early parts of the twentieth century, I mean the right to vote and so on. Then there was a second women's movement in the 1960s and the 1970s that was about getting rid of all the rules, regulations, customs and habits that concretely excluded women from access to all sorts of areas. The second women's movement tried to turn abstract rights into concrete rights. But that is still talking about *rights*. Assuming that we can build on the gains of these two waves of feminist activism, we now need to do something about *concrete participation* in all areas of life. That's what I call 'access to the universal'. American women have long had equal rights to participation in political life. Yet only 14 per cent of the members of the US Congress are women, I think. We then get a debate about *why this is so*? Conservatives say, 'It's women's free choice. Women just aren't so interested in politics.' People on the left, like myself, say it's all about ideology, social practices and so on.

There was a story in the *New York Times* recently about the relatively low number of women candidates in the Parliamentary elections in France this year, in spite of the new laws on *parité*. Some French male politician quoted in the *New York Times* said something like this: 'Oh well, there are many women elected on the local level, on the municipal level. You know women are more interested in the local, in the close things. They don't take such an interest in the large political problems.' Blatant sexism. Such generalization about women's interests encroaches on women's freedom, it is a form of brainwashing that tells women what they should be interested in.

So, to put it very briefly, I think that for women in developed Western societies the process of modernization that started with the French Revolution isn't finished yet. Though we now have abstract equal rights, we certainly don't have them concretely in the sense of women really participating equally in all social spheres. This is linked to what I was saying at the very beginning of our conversation about women not having access to the universal – if 'universal' just means the general category. It seems to me that 'the general', or 'the norm' is still defined as masculine, and women who try to break into it are in trouble in various ways. What we need is society to be transformed to make it easier for women actually to participate in all kinds of activities and to choose them freely. And, of course, right now the biggest problem for women in the United States has to do with the way in which family life, child care and work are organized. Only for women who have a lot of money is it reasonably easy to have small children and a demanding job at the same time. The same is not true for men. In the US today it is even more difficult to be a poor woman with children. Equal participation in all social spheres for women can't become a reality if it doesn't also mean equal participation in parenting by both sexes.

Michael Payne: I want to give you just one name in the context of this particular feminist theme, which we are not calling any longer 'cultural contingency' but rather 'cultural specificity'. You may not even want to talk about this scholar's work because it comes from outside the traditions we've been discussing, but I'm thinking about Martha Nussbaum and a book like *Sex and Social Justice*. Here she's working with both liberalism and humanism as well as making use of not only legal cases but also her own particular experience in India. But I don't think she's somebody who many people would think of as a feminist in any sense.

Toril Moi: My problem with Nussbaum is that she works with a far too Millsean, or liberal idea of responsibility. She underestimates the difficulties of freedom, because she doesn't really have a sufficiently complex theory of human subjectivity. For instance, in *Women and Human Development,* published in 2000, the year after *Sex and Social Justice*, she spends an awful lot of time on the idea of writing constitutions and on the situation of women in India. The problem is that India has long had a radical, egalitarian constitution. Yet this doesn't seem to have helped women in India much. Nussbaum overlooks the complex network of social and personal forces that make it impossible for people to choose freedom, even if they rationally ought to.

As to whether Nussbaum is a feminist: why not call her that? Feminism should be a very broad church indeed. I don't know whether Nussbaum herself would call herself a feminist, but she certainly is pro-women. There are some political and legal theorists who work with a far too rational model of subjectivity. That makes their results suspect. I mean that they tend to equate the human subject with pure rationality. Although Nussbaum has written intelligently about emotions, she remains too much in that 'rationalist' camp for my taste. That's probably one reason why a lot of what she says isn't having a broad impact among literary theorists, who simply don't think like that about subjectivity.

Michael Payne: Her work is certainly very much focused on the United Nations' declaration of universal human rights rather than, as you say, any sense of the immediate facticity – specificity – of people's everyday cultural experience.

Toril Moi: Well, you see, I am actually totally in favour of the universal declaration of human rights. That kind of thing is necessary if women are to get 'access to the universal'. I want to *build* on the achievements of previous generations of feminists, not reject them. Abstract declarations are not enough, however. I want to think about how to make such general principles become a concrete reality in human life. Which means thinking about all the thick, complex layers of lived experience, of ideologies and practices, that makes us what we are. If we don't work on this, declarations and constitutions are just part of an irrelevant, idealist superstructure, to put it that way.

Michael Payne: Ok, let's come back from Nussbaum to Toril Moi. Your recent unpublished essay, 'Meaning What We Say' very obviously echoes Stanley Cavell's famous 1958 essay 'Must We Mean What We Say?' In your essay, there are a number of allusions to Cavell as well as moments where you actually make use of his thinking. One of his continuing themes is, of course, acknowledgement or its opposite: disowning. And what he keeps emphasizing is that there is an important aspect of scepticism that's not just a problem of knowledge but also a problem of how we affirm and act on what we know. Now, the other part of your title is 'The Responsibility of Intellectuals', and that seems to echo Noam Chomsky, Edward Said and Bertrand Russell, all of whom have written on the public responsibility of intellectuals. So, what I want to ask you is whether, in terms of your own work, there is a cumulative speech-act of some kind? In other words, what is it that you want your writing *to do*?

Toril Moi: I think we all write to *do* something. Ultimately, of course, I write to promote and increase women's freedom. But that can be done in myriad ways. More specifically, I would say my project is to encourage young women, in particular, to find a voice of their own, so as to be able to say what they mean, in whatever context they find themselves. That is part of what women need to do to get access to the universal. Finding a voice is a key theme for me with Cavell. Cavell's book, *Contesting Tears: The Melodrama of the Unknown Woman* has been very important to me because it helps me to theorize the difficulty for a woman of finding a voice.

Beauvoir says that to write is to 'appeal to the other's freedom'. I think that's a beautiful way of putting it. I can't force people to read me, or agree with me. All I can do is to write as well and as clearly as I can about the things that matter to me, in the hope that I can show why they should matter to others too. This is to write with the *ambition* of the universal, to speak with Cavell.

Another thing I aim to do – this should be quite obvious – is to keep a strong feminist tradition alive both in the intellectual world and in the academy because it is, by no means, assured. It's so fragile. As I said at the outset of our conversation, look at what is called theory these days; and how women and feminism (not the same thing) are once again marginalized subjects. In my own work I draw on a very broad range of theories by men as well as women. I would like men to do the same.

Michael Payne: Before we finish, I would like to ask for any thoughts you might want to communicate on the subject of globalization in relation to feminism. I am thinking, in part, of Hardt and Negri's recent book *Empire*, which made a big splash when it first appeared, though it seems almost to have disappeared from view. I don't know if that's because of 9/11 and its aftermath, or what; however, my question is this: Is the critique of globalization important for feminism? And has that issue in some ways moved into the space where Beauvoir's socialism was before?

Toril Moi: Well, the thing about globalization theory (or, at least, what I have read of it so far) is that, like modernity theory, once again none of the major theorists has actually bothered to talk about women or women's situation. So, again a feminist theorist is in a position where the first thing to be done is to figure out where to place women in these theories. But is it worth it? Or is the theory so muddleheaded with regard to gender that we'd better start somewhere else? It is not clear that women *can* just pick up current globalization theory and run with it. Just like other theorists, globalization theorists fail to make sex and gender a fundamental part of their theory. In my travels around the world I have found that a lot of women in many different countries are very interested in hearing something that addresses the possibility of women's freedom and self-determination. Now, this possibility can be formulated in many theoretical idioms. I challenge the people, not least the men, who do globalization theory to engage with these questions.

Michael Payne: You mention that you have met many women all around the world who are responsive to feminism in one form or another; could you say a little more about that?

Toril Moi: Beauvoir, for example, is of great interest to many non-Western women. Only last year there was a new Chinese translation of *The Second Sex*. I'm really struck by that, particularly when one Western criticism of Beauvoir has been that she is so ethnocentric, that she is only interested in the French. A good feminist theory should be addressed to the other's freedom. That other is not supposed to be just Western or just non-Western women. It should be a challenge to everyone. That doesn't mean that everyone will agree with it or find it useful, but that everyone should feel invited to enter into discussion with it. To write is to say as clearly as possible *what* I think and *why*, and then present it to 'the other'. And 'the other' here includes anyone who might want to read it, whether they be women in Korea and India, or in Norway and England. The gesture we make – or that we ought to make – when we write is the one that says: 'This is how I see it. Can you see it too?' And if they *can't* see it, they should correct it, that is to say, find their own voices, and speak back. That, for me, is what it means to write with the *ambition* of the universal. Writing should be dialogic activity in which you're trying to reach insights other people can share. You may fail, but that's what you're reaching for.

Toril Moi: We certainly shouldn't believe that we are in any position to tell other people what they *should* be interested in. What we can do, is to analyse how our own and other people's interests arise, how they are shaped and produced by social, cultural and personal factors. When I speak of writing with the ambition of the universal, I obviously don't mean that Western women or feminists should go out there and evangelize, but that all women should try to find their voices and say what they think, in a way that makes it possible for others to respond. We should also show what it is that prevents women in different situations from speaking up for themselves.

Michael Payne: Thank you. Is there anything that we haven't talked about that you'd like to address?

Toril Moi: Well, there is one small thing I'd like to add. You talk about 'life *after* theory', but we should not forget that the 1980s' sense of 'theory' still reigns supreme, at least in the United States. It still produces the paradigm for most postgraduate education in literature in the USA today. But if we ask if 'theory' today is still a source of new and original work, then the answer is no. There is an awful lot of derivative and second-rate work out there. 'Theory' today is the orthodoxy, the dogma that's taught to every student. If you want to be a really radical student today, one that annoys the professors terribly, you can just start claiming that words have meanings. What I and many other people have been trying quietly to do for the last ten years is to find different ways of thinking, ways that make sense to me and that allow me to say something that I can *believe in*, that I can *mean*. And I have found this, in different ways, by confronting my post-structuralist heritage with thinkers like Wittgenstein, Austin and Cavell. (Don't, though, get me started on the way poststructuralists read these thinkers – we could have another, very long conversation about that.) I certainly have got a lot out of reading outside the French theory tradition. But whatever way people choose to go, the point is to stop repeating a hegemonic and increasingly dogmatic discourse. It is important to find a voice of one's own.

epilogue

coming back to 'life': 'Leavis spells pianos'

John Schad

'life' is a necessary word

F. R. Leavis[1]

To talk of 'life' after theory is, in a sense, to *come back* to life since we have been there before, before theory, with F. R. Leavis, the Cambridge critic who from the forties to the sixties dominated literary criticism with his reverential and enigmatic talk of 'life'. For Leavis, 'every creative writer of the greatest kind knows that in a major work he is developing thought – thought about life'.[2] To this day, within literary criticism, 'life' means Leavis and Leavis means 'life'; if though, after theory, we may be allowed to invoke a clumsy and eccentric detail of Leavis's *own* life, we find that 'Leavis Spells Pianos', that being the slogan by which Leavis's father used to advertise the pianos he made and sold in Edwardian Cambridge.[3] Of course, if, for literary criticism, 'life' is a necessary word, 'piano' is a supremely *un*necessary word, a word that does not follow; but it is for that very reason that it *is* necessary in that it recalls us to the simple fact that our thinking about a text does not always make sense, or at least common sense, and yet in so doing immediately makes *un*common sense – for criticism or theory *does* (if we think about it) have a fragile but curious relationship to the piano. On the

168

front cover of a recent Derrida text the theorist appears, almost ironically, seated with his back to an upright drawing-room piano; in 'Circumfession' (1991), where he appears seated at his computer, Derrida talks knowingly of 'playing the keyboard'.[4] Almost twenty years before, Derrida's friend Roland Barthes glances at the 'history of the piano' and declares:

> we know that today post-serial music has radically altered the role of the 'interpreter', who is called on to be ... the co-author of the score. The text is very much a score of this new kind: it asks of the reader a practical collaboration.[5]

There is, it seems, something about the twentieth-century piano that lends itself to a radical or writerly account of the reader as player, or improviser. Valentine Cunningham is right, there *is* a tacit relationship between poststructuralism and jazz – it is no accident that Derrida did, on one occasion, write a text for accompaniment on jazz-piano. [6] Theorists and critics did not, though, need to wait for jazz, or even post-serial music, before they first thought of themselves as artists; all they needed was a piano. As early as 1890 Oscar Wilde gave us the 'The Critic as Artist', a comic Socratic dialogue between two characters or voices called Earnest and Gilbert; if Barthes is a theorist *on* the piano then Gilbert is the theorist *at* the piano: the dialogue opens with the splendid Gilbert seated, quite literally, 'at the piano'. As the dialogue proceeds Gilbert, when not offering to 'play Chopin ... or Dvořák', advances an effortless and paradoxical overturning of Matthew Arnold's famous essay 'The Function of Criticism at the

Present Time' (1864). While, for the commonsensical Arnold, the critic is secondary to the author, for Gilbert it is the critic who is the true artist; moreover, while for Arnold the true function of criticism is 'to see the object as in itself it really is', for Gilbert it is, naturally, 'to see the object as in itself it really is *not*'.[7]

The view from the piano is – as one might expect – no view at all, it is all about the art of *not* seeing, of *mis*-reading, of not doing 'proper' literary criticism at all; Gilbert, we sense, would rather be playing Chopin. This view, or non-view was, in fact, put straight to Leavis himself when in 1929 he received a visit from the philosopher Wittgenstein, a man who had grown up in a house of seven pianos; apropos absolutely nothing, or 'without prelude' – as Leavis notes – Wittgenstein declared: 'Give up literary criticism!'[8] Academic literary criticism no sooner begins than it is told to give up; it is, from the beginning, marked with what Kermode has taught us to call a 'sense of an ending', its own ending. Theory, of course, has in very various ways renewed this sense of crisis; at times, it too implies there may be better things to do than literary criticism. The deconstructionist, one senses, would rather be doing philosophy – this, of course, would take us back to Gilbert who spends a whole night theorizing about criticism but never actually does any. Again, the New Historicist or cultural materialist, one senses, would rather be doing history, *doing life*, as it were, or *the real*. This, curiously, might just take us back to that would-be 'Professor of Life' (as Woolf called him), Sir Walter Raleigh, the Oxford Professor of English Literature who was quite open about the fact that he could not wait to give up literary criticism for something more active, or vital – an ambition that he finally realized with the onset of the First World War.[9] To make fun of Raleigh is easy (and indeed fun) but, after theory, we may just share, almost without knowing it, something of his conviction that there is more to life than 'English Literature'. It is true that Leavis protected us from this sense, convincing many both inside and outside universities that academic English almost *is* life; as Eagleton writes, 'by the early 1930s ... English [Literature] was ... [considered] *the* supremely civilizing pursuit'.[10] Now of course, like Raleigh, we are not so sure; partly because, after Auschwitz, we are not sure what civilization is and partly because theory is, above all, an opening of English to other disciplines. Theory is, in a sense, a way of taking Wittgenstein's advice; quite literally, in the case of Christopher Norris – 'Mr Norris', as Empson called him, recently changed not trains but departments, Philosophy for English.[11]

Others, though, cannot give up; after 50 years of literary criticism, Frank Kermode is still 'doing this kind of thing'.[12] Likewise, Derrida has never wholly given up literature for philosophy, his lecture on perjury was primarily, as he stressed, a reading of a novel. As T. S. Eliot wrote, 'criticism is as inevitable as breathing'[13] – he was right, even after theory, criticism can still mean life. What may have changed, however, is that theory has reminded us that life itself means death, that living is a form of dying. This has much to do with the turn to Freud for whom, of course, 'the end of all life is death'. It also has much to do with Derrida who almost evokes the medieval *memento mori* tradition; for Derrida, life and death constitute yet another impossible binary: 'it is, already, *life death*', he writes[14] – or, as very different theorists would say, life for one often comes at the expense of death for another, *the* other. Indeed, it is the argument of Paul de Man *et al.*, that such killing is carried out in the *name* of Life, that at the dead centre of ideology, at the dead centre of all the ways in which we blind ourselves to the difference, or otherness of the other, is the myth of the organic whole. To dream of the One, of the whole, has often meant drawing on notions of organic unity – as Derrida observes, in Hegel

> the absolute Idea in its infinite truth is still determined as Life, true life, absolute life, life without death, imperishable life, the life of truth.[15]

The dangers of such absolute, or total Life are obvious; we cannot forget that in the 1930s Leavis was not the only one to talk of 'life' – when Nazi Germany invaded Eastern Europe they did so because Hitler had developed the theory of *Lebensraum*, meaning 'life-space', or 'living-room' for a greater Germany. This is not, of course, to suggest that Leavis was drawing on Hegel or was complicit with the extreme nationalism of his day, it is simply that theory has made us wary of the idea of Life, or indeed any other organicist master-word. The organic, though, need not always serve Hegelian ends; as Kermode points out, when the German Romantics thought of the work of art in organic terms it entailed a sense of the inevitable decay and dissolution within nature.[16] Life is not necessarily whole; this, in fact, is Derrida's point when, in *Glas* (1974), he looks at the divided 'structure of the flower', at what the botanists call dehiscence, and remarks that 'life and division go together'.[17] Theory, it is often thought, 'murders to dissect' but for the Derrida of *Glas* it is life that does the dissecting – 'deconstruction of the transcendental effect', he writes, 'is at work in the structure of the flower'. Strangely, in Derrida the familiar poststructural stress on difference arises from not only linguistics but botany, not only the library but the garden. In this respect deconstruction is a kind of life-writing; it is, though, life implicated in death, or *thanatos* – hence Derrida's conceitful talk of his 'auto*biothanato*heterographical opus'.[18]

This outrageous neologism comes from Derrida's 'Circumfession', a strange mix of memoir and meditation; here theory becomes life-writing in the sense of autobiography. But then theory has always had a secret autobiographical life; the very people who brought us 'The Death of the Author' have also had the nerve to bring us 'The Life of the Theorist' – witness, not only 'Circumfession' but also *Roland Barthes by Roland Barthes* (1975), and Althusser's *The Future Lasts a Long Time* (1992). This irony would not, though, surprise Gilbert, the paradoxical theorist at the piano; for, with unswerving hyperbole, Gilbert announces that 'Criticism . . . is the only civilized form of autobiography.' And this is so, it seems, even when the criticism itself disavows the personal; take the case of Foucault, who

declares that he 'writes in order to have no face' and yet
admits that 'I have always wanted my books to be
fragments from an autobiography'.[19] Foucault does not,
of course, say *whose* autobiography – perhaps, it is
'everybody's autobiography', a phrase of Gertrude
Stein's that fascinates Derrida; and Derrida it is who,
with a perversity worthy of Gilbert, coolly remarks that
' "autobiography" is perhaps the least inadequate name'
for 'what interests me'.[20] This may come as something of
a surprise, but if true then deconstruction is life but not
as we know it from conventional life-writing, deconstruction is hardly 'a civilized form of autobiography'.
Instead, it is life as Derrida knows it from Walter Benjamin, life as something resistant to the smooth con-
tinuities of civilization; Benjamin is the German-Jewish
refugee who – just months before killing himself to
avoid a still worse fate at the hands of the Nazis – writes
that in order to 'blast open the continuum of history'
one must 'blast ... a specific life out of the era'.[21] Thirty
years later Benjamin's blasted life is echoed by de Man
when he writes that 'any attempt at a total understanding of our being (*Wesen*) will stand in contrast to
actual ... fragmentary, particular and unfulfilled life
(*Leben*)'.[22] There is, though, an obvious irony here; for
de Man's own life – one part writer for collaborationist
newspaper in occupied Belgium, another part arch-
theorist at Yale – was so fragmented, so divided as to
disrupt a total understanding of not just 'being' but
deconstruction; de Man's double life blasts open not just
the continuum of history but the continuum of theory.
The dramatic discovery in 1987 of de Man's wartime

journalism rudely interrupted the American dream of deconstruction as 'the joyous affirmation of the play of the world and of the innocence of becoming'.[23] These words come from Derrida at Baltimore in 1966, he is describing what he calls the Nietzschean 'side of the thinking of play'; after the de Man affair, never again such innocence. Almost overnight (or so it now seems) theory discovered itself to be, in a sense, a post-war event, or trauma – an attempt to deal with dark European memories. Admittedly, this had been hinted at; as early as 1984 Eagleton spoke better then he knew when he remarked, of deconstruction's absolute scepticism of any system of thought, that

> behind the … Yale School would seem to loom … [the] shadow of the holocaust. Harold Bloom is a Jew, Geoffrey Hartman is of central European Jewish provenance; de Man's uncle … was politically involved in the Second World War period. [24]

Once de Man's own political involvement was known there was, it seems, no escaping the Second World War; indeed, in Derrida's work we seem still to be at war, even when in California, where in 1993 he remarked: 'it is still evening, it is always nightfall along the "ramparts", on the battlements of an old Europe at war'.[25]

I. A. Richards once suggested that Leavis' veneration for 'Life' was part of a wider preoccupation with the word among those who, like Leavis himself, witnessed for themselves the many deaths of the First Word War. [26] To suggest that theory is, in its turn, a response to the Second World War is, in fact, to say that theory is 'life' in the strict etymological sense of the word – for 'life' comes from the prehistoric German *lib* meaning 'remain' or 'be left' and, as one dictionary puts it, 'the semantic connection between '"remaining" and *life* ... is thought to lie in the notion of being "left alive after a battle"'.[27] If life is, necessarily, *after*-life; if all living is a form of 'living–*on*', in particular living-on after war, then theory is very much a form of life. Not only do Bloom, Hartman and Derrida belong to a generation of Jews that was ravaged by the Holocaust but when Lacan's wife declared herself Jewish he went personally to the Gestapo to retrieve her dossier, thereby almost certainly saving her life. There is also Althusser who never forgot the experience of being a prisoner of war, and Foucault who invokes the 'sight[s] we had known during the German occupation'.[28]

If the generation of post-war French intellectuals that gave us theory are, by definition, survivors then Derrida is a survivor of the survivors since he has lived to see life *after* theory. In the last twenty years Derrida has on at least fourteen occasions written texts in memory of dead colleagues: from Barthes in 1980 to Lyotard in 1998; enough writing to fill, quite literally, a whole book, or work of mourning.[29] At Lyotard's funeral Derrida remarks,

> I seem to recall having [recently] said that ... Jean-François ... and I [are] the sole survivors of ... a 'generation' – of which I am the last born, and, no doubt, the most melancholic .... What can I say today, then? That I love Jean-François, that I miss him.[30]

Derrida, it seems, could almost be speaking of himself when he cites Fontanier's strangely 'pathetic and human' definition of the anacoluthon as 'letting stand alone a word that calls out for another as companion. This missing companion is no longer a *companion*.'[31] Theory, if personified by Derrida, is what Fontanier calls a 'wanting sentence'; life after theory, or at the end of theory thus answers to a grammatical definition. The last laugh, or last sigh, belongs perhaps to de Man, he who (in)famously declared that 'death is a displaced name for a linguistic predicament'.[32] If so, de Man returns even as he departs.

This, as it happens, is very nearly the logic of Derrida's remark that 'Paul de Man *was* my friend. Paul de Man *is* my friend.'[33] Here, though, de Man does not quite return as he left; Paul de Man the new, posthumous friend is not the same as Paul de Man the old, living friend – the posthumous friend has a guilty past and is, therefore, someone whom Derrida never quite knew while alive. This coming and going – or rather going and coming – is, in fact, inscribed in Derrida's extended account of 'anacoluthonic discontinuity'; for though it leaves you lacking the companion you expected it also gives you a companion you did not expect – to quote Derrida's lecture:

> In life ... I [cannot] foresee change ... I [can]not foresee *who*, *the other* who has arrived in the interval.

For Derrida, the anacoluthon entails the possibility of a *new* companion, 'the sudden arrival of another person'.[34] But then we should know this, for the most famously interrupted text in English Literature is, of course, Coleridge's 'Kubla Khan', a transcription of a dream that is forever abandoned following the strange and sudden arrival of an unidentified 'person on business from Porlock'.[35] There is more to anacoluthon than simply lack, and this secret is buried in the very word 'companion', the word on which both Fontanier and Derrida insist and which, if broken open, reveals '*companis*' meaning 'with-bread' – a companion is, literally, one with whom you share bread; and, of course, the most famous sharer of bread is Jesus, he who, on returning to life, appeared to two friends on a road who only recognized him when he broke and shared bread – in that instant he immediately disappeared:

> And it came to pass, as he sat at meat with them, he took bread, and blessed it, and brake, and gave to them. And their eyes were opened, and they knew him; and he vanished out of their sight. (Luke 24.30–1)

Here, in the very moment of becoming a com-panion, Jesus not only plays the interruptive, anacoluthonic role of leaving others alone but he also, and at the same time, reveals himself; he both comes and goes in the same moment of com-panionship. The expected, predictable, figure leaves – the man they had met on the road – and a wholly unexpected figure arrives, the man they would call God.

All this recalls Kermode's observation, apropos theory, that 'the door that was opened in the late 1960s let in many unexpected visitors';[36] perhaps the most unexpected visitor has been – as for those men on the road – the enigmatic and almost embarrassing figure of God. 'Leave the door open to ... Elijah,' suggests Derrida in 1977. For Lacan, indeed, writing in1975, 'God has [never] ... made his exit.'[37] Cixous, Irigaray and Kristeva have also all made major and obvious contributions to theory's theological turn, a turn that has been both dramatic and conspicuous.[38] It is, though, for many a turn for the worse; in this volume Christopher Norris expresses a disquiet that is shared, I guess, by many of theory's early enthusiasts, most of whom belonged to a profoundly secular, even secularist, generation, parti-cularly in the UK where the greatest impetus for theory came – as Toril Moi recalls in her interview – from the Left, from critics committed to materialist, or empiricist modes of thought.

It is true, of course, that Anglo-American criticism has traditionally styled itself as a would-be religion, as a discipline that only just falls short of the realm of the spirit; as late as 1982 Kermode could write that

> the history of criticism ... is a history of ... attempts to earn the privilege of access to that kingdom of the larger existence which is in our time the secular surrogate of another king-dom whose existence is no longer within our range.[39]

This is not far from many a remark in Derrida's more recent work, his work on the question of spirit; but what distinguishes the two is Kermode's insistence on the secular/sacred opposition. Elsewhere Kermode expands on this, arguing that 'secularization multiplies the world's structures of probability';[40] with secularization,

Kermode suggests, there are more stories rather than less but he is also saying, in effect, that the secularized world is not, as we usually think, a more contingent and anarchic place but rather a place *full of probabilities* – in short, a *more* predictable place. This is nowhere more obvious than in Anglo-American literary criticism whose characteristic empiricism has very obviously made for more probability, pattern and rule than in the texts of high and, as it were, high-Spirited French theory. Empiricist criticism, we might say, tends not to expect the unexpected, is less expectant of surprise; however, ironically, it is for precisely this reason that such criticism is all the more *vulnerable* to surprise, in particular to the surprise of the spirit. It is not Derrida but Kermode who describes reading as 'the blindman's bluff of the spirit' and it is Anglo-American criticism rather than French theory that has been most consistently marked by the true surprise of the spirit, which is not so much to be (as Wordsworth would have it) 'surprised by joy' but rather (as Stanley Fish would have it) 'surprised by sin', or injustice.[41] For some thirty years English Studies has at least heard (if not heeded) the very various critiques of feminists, Marxists, postcolonialists and queer theorists; these critiques, though once informed by such as Foucault and Althusser, have increasingly returned to the moral and political roots of English to read much literature and indeed criticism as ideological, as silently complicit with the operation of power and privilege. What has been at work is a hermeneutics of suspicion in which the object of suspicion is, in part, hermeneutics itself, or rather the institutionalization of hermeneutics that is academic English. The criticism that has raged against this establishment has been, at best, a form of institutional confession, an admission of collective, and structural guilt.

We are not, of course, accustomed to think of criticism as confessional; however, one of the surprises of theory is its intuition that *all* criticism entails an admission of guilt. After all, if no one can ever mean exactly what they say then the critic too is doomed to perjury: 'one always asks for pardon when one writes' (Derrida); again, if everything is always already written then all writing is a form of theft: 'I didn't earn my book by the sweat of my brow ... I stole [it]' (Cixous); and, yet again, if the birth of the reader requires the death of the author then all reading is a form of murder: 'right here I kill you' (Derrida again). [42] 'We are,' Derrida adds, 'the worst criminals in history', and so we are if we accept his Levinasian account of ethics as responsibility to the other:

> in ethics ... responsibility ... is infinite ... that's why I always feel guilty.[43]

Back in 1971, at the beginning of theory, Barthes declared that 'the Text cannot stop',[44] a phrase that for many announced the endless and unbounded play of meaning; however, by the end of theory it seems as if *responsibility* cannot stop. This logic, or illogic, is pushed to its hyperbolic extreme when Derrida, in 1992, remarks that

> by preferring my work ... as a ... philosopher ... I am sacrificing and betraying at every moment all my other

obligations: my obligations to the other others ... the billions
of my fellows, my fellows who are dying of starvation and
disease.[45]

This, of course, is easy to say and impossible to mean; it
is, though, also difficult to forget, for the reality of
'third-world' starvation is so absolute in its awfulness
that if the activity of reading and writing about books is
to mean anything, is to be in any sense a responsible
activity, then it must somehow connect with that star-
ving. In the instant we recognize this we are alerted to
the unbearable heaviness of being a reader.

In the very same instant, however, we are also alerted
to the unbearable *lightness* of being a reader, for if we
are persuaded – if only for a moment – by Derrida's
sense of infinite responsibility, by this ethical version of
Freud's conviction that 'everything is related to everything',[46] then we might also be persuaded (or at least
infected) by Barthes's sense of infinite textual play, or
freedom. As usual, responsibility and freedom are related; as Derrida writes, 'There are ethics [in reading]
because there is no rule ... because I don't know what to
do';[47] reading is weighed down with responsibility
because it is so free. Reading's heaviness is also its
lightness; responsibility does not stop because *the text*
does not stop. If this is so, if every text is indeed related
to every other text, then my interpretative choices are
forever haunted by the possibility that they could be
otherwise, that they are, in some sense, contingent or
arbitrary. In this connection, Kermode once asked the
question 'Can We Say Absolutely Anything We Like?'

and in a sense, or in theory, perhaps we *can*.[48] As Derrida argues, 'the space of literature ... in principle allows one to say everything/anything [*tout dire*]' – that is, in part, the point of literature. Again, this is no weightless freedom since, for Derrida, it is 'inseparable ... from what calls forth a democracy'; this freedom, however, is also inseparable from what Derrida describes as 'bewilderment', or 'a feeling of existence as excess, "being superfluous"'. Tellingly, Derrida here quotes Sartre and he too, back in 1947, saw literature as freedom: 'the work of art, from which ever side you approach it, is an act of confidence in the freedom of men'.[49] For Sartre, though, this freedom is *too much*; with neither God, nor even human nature to determine existence Man is *too* free, 'he ... is *condemned* to be free'.[50] Looking back to Sartre – as Toril Moi might applaud – Derrida sees the freedom that is literature as not only blessing but curse, an aspect of the nauseous lightness of reading.

This lightness is never felt more than whenever I find that my mind has wandered in the very act of reading; I am still 'reading' (in an automatic, senseless sense) but I am not thinking about it. To echo Derrida's refrain, 'Just imagine, I was not thinking about it,'[51] or at least not always. And that, argues Derrida, is our fate even when we *think* we are thinking about it; for Derrida, there is always 'the possibility ... threat or chance of ... forgetting, the effects of an irreducible distraction at the heart of finite thought'.[52] It is true, as Kermode observes, that much theory is thinking about thinking about books,[53] but sometimes theory is thinking about *not* thinking about books. Hence Derrida's question 'What is called not thinking?' and, if you like, Lacan's answer which is, quite simply: *being, being* human – Lacan declares, 'I think where I am not, therefore I am where I do not think.'[54] Lacan, of course, is inverting that most fundamental philosophical axiom, Descartes's 'I think therefore I am'; and in much the same anti-philosophical way Derrida's question is a disruption of the title of Heidegger's essay, 'What is Called Thinking?'[55] But then the title disrupts itself in the sense that the original German, *Was Heisst Denken?* can also mean 'What Calls for Thinking?' implying that something prior to thinking lies beyond, or ahead of thinking, a something that thinking is after, or in pursuit of. For theory, it seems, that *something* is 'not thinking', *that* is what theory is after. Hence Derrida's concern to 'bring back non-memory to memory', or Pierre Macherey's pursuit of 'the unconscious' of the text.[56]

Other theorists have reflected this same concern with not thinking by attempting to think that which *cannot* be thought or indeed by thinking that which simply *is not*. Witness Foucault's fascination with 'the madman's speech ... [that does] not exist'; Irigaray's riddling account of 'the second sex' as 'this sex which is not one'; and Lacan's claim that, in language, 'Nothing exists except in so far it does not exist.'[57] If all these negatives have a single 'origin' it is, of course, the structuralist claim that a word only signifies by virtue of its difference from every other word. Ferdinand de Saussure argues that 'what characterizes each [sign] most exactly is being whatever the others are not'; or, as Eagleton puts it, 'every sign is what it is because it is not all the other signs'.[58] Each word, we might say, is haunted by every other word, by all that it is not – it is haunted, in other words, *by everything else*; if so, the sombre 'not', or 'no' of Saussure's differential account of language entails the wild 'yes' of everything else. And that is precisely what poststructuralism picks up on; as Derrida demonstrates when he writes 'What deconstruction is not? Everything of course !'[59]

This returns us, of course, to the theorist at the piano, to Gilbert's perverse insistence that the task of criticism is 'to see the thing in itself as it really is not'; after theory, we might say the task is to see the thing in itself as *everything else* it is not. And that is precisely what Lacan does when he finds, in Saussure's text, the diagram of a tree and, in a self-parodic tour de force (or farce) of quite spectacular overreading, sees not the poor tree but instead:

> the cross ... the capital Y ... the sign of dichotomy ... [the] circulatory tree, [the] tree of life of the cerebellum, tree of Saturn, tree of Diana, crystals formed in a tree struck by lightning, is it your figure that traces our destiny for us in the tortoiseshell cracked by the fire, or your lightning that causes that slow shift in the axis of being to surge up from an unnameable night into the Ἐν πάντα [one in all] of language:
>
> *No! says the Tree, it says No! in the shower of sparks*
> *Of its superb head*
>
> Paul-Ambroise Valéry[60]

The protest of Valéry's tree is, in a sense, the protest of the thing in itself as it really is; the protest is telling, resonant, even tragic – Lacan allows it and hears it but it is, finally, ignored. Lacan, of course, is by no means the first to ignore it. Even I.A. Richards, that most scientific of critics, insisted that a tree in a poem 'is *not* a tree';[61] but then this was in 1924 at the height of literary modernism, a movement that was determined to 'make it new', to see the thing *not* as it is in a mirror or a realist novel. In this sense, much theory is *belated* modernism; indeed, Gregory Ulmer argues that poststructuralism is to the history of literary criticism what modernism is to the history of art:

> the break with 'mimesis', with the values and assumptions of 'realism', which revolutionised the modernist arts, is now underway (belatedly) in criticism.[62]

As we know, Lacan drew very deliberately on one particular school of modernism: namely, surrealism; and there is a sense in which the true legacy of theory is, in part, surrealist. Hence Hayden White's immodest proposal that literary historians might pursue 'the possibility of using ... surrealists' modes of representation'.[63]

   To do so, of course, would entail the possibility of laughter, but if theory has taught us anything it is that critical thought, however sublime, may never be far from the ridiculous. Witness not only Lacan's hermeneutic overkilling of Saussure's poor tree but also Derrida's *Spurs*, in which Derrida offers, with almost exaggerated seriousness, a profound philosophic meditation upon the words, 'I forgot my umbrella.'[64] Paul de Man once wrote that 'the impossibility of reading should not be taken too lightly' but he forgot to add that it should also not be taken too seriously.[65] At its best, theory makes us profoundly aware of the gravity of reading without our mistaking gravity for seriousness. In 'Envois', in defence of Oxford scholasticism, Derrida writes, 'it's ... grave and dangerous ... but not serious' – that is why he likes it; a little further, apropos something else (but just imagine it is theory), Derrida writes, 'it is [still] the sacred, for me ... but as such it also makes me laugh, it does leave us laughter, thank God'.[66] It also leaves us Oscar Wilde, thank God; for part of 'Envois' – an epistolary essay centred on Oxford – is 'thought for Oscar Wilde',[67] that tragi-comic Oxonian who was so often grave and dangerous but never serious. What theory leaves behind may yet prove to be comedy, an appreciation of what Kierkegaard called 'the strength of the absurd'.[68] If so, Wilde is a key figure. It is no accident that in the 1970s Eagleton was working towards a Machereyean 'science of the text' but by the late 1980s was writing a comic stage play on the life and death of one he calls 'St Oscar'. After theory *is*, in a sense, Gilbert; here is not so much the critic as artist but what Eagleton elsewhere calls 'the critic as clown',[69] or even *piss* artist, for though Gilbert sits at the piano offering to play Chopin he scarcely seems to touch the piano; in this sense, he comes closer to playing John Cage's infamous *4 minutes and 33 seconds* in which the pianist sits solemnly before a closed piano while the audience hears *everything but the piano*. Cage's pianist demonstrates, in a sense, what Gilbert believes is the 'importance of doing nothing';[70] for Gilbert, it seems, unless we do nothing with the text, unless we are distracted from it, see it as it really is not, we cannot hear the roar of everything else – or what Lacan calls 'the real', that 'noise in which everything can be heard'.[71]

If Matthew Arnold was concerned with what he calls 'the function of criticism' then Gilbert, we might say, is concerned with the criticism of function. He teaches us a lesson also taught by theory: namely, that if the text (like the sign) is what it is *not* then in order to read the text we should read everything but the text. We might well call this New Historicism, or doing cultural history – whatever, it is patently absurd, not serious. It is, though, both grave and dangerous for it involves a gamble or risk, the risk of losing not just the text but ourselves. This, of course – as Toril Moi might stress – is the existential condition, what Heidegger calls 'the high and dangerous game and gamble in which, by the essence of language, we are the stakes'.[72] And so we are, or should be; for if we really are to read the text as the everything it is not then we might just become, in a sense, *everybody* we are not. Witness Cixous's vision of the woman that 'is ... capable of others, of the other woman that she will be, of the other woman she isn't, of him, of you'.[73] Note too that Derrida, echoing James Joyce, cries 'Here Comes Everybody' and dreams, as we know, of writing 'Everybody's Autobiography'.[74]

If to read after theory is to be left with everybody but ourselves then we may just be nearer to something we would call truth; as Derrida remarks, 'when *we* are present, the truth is not there'[75] – we frighten it away. This for Derrida, is part of the illogic of the anacoluthon, according to which we can never be in the company of the truth about ourselves; we are always, in Fontanier's words, 'left standing alone without companion'. But, of course, to be without com-panion, without one-to-share-bread-with, is to discover as new companion (or rather, new double or demon) anyone who has no bread to share simply because *they have no bread at all*. This, in a sense, is what Derrida calls 'the *companionship* ... of ghosts'.[76] We may yet be alarmed by what comes back to life after theory.

> *Like ghosts amid your palaces*
> *Thoughts of poor men force their way*

Ernest Jones, 'We are Silent,' 1851[77]

Notes

CHAPTER 1 FOLLOWING THEORY: JACQUES DERRIDA

1   Henri Thomas, *Le parjure* (Paris: Gallimard, 1964) p. 134.
2   See Browning's poem, 'St Martin's Summer'.
3   See Derrida and Vattimo (eds), *Religion* (Cambridge: Polity,1998) pp. 1–78.
4   Jacques Derrida, *Acts of Religion*, ed. Gil Anidjar (London: Routledge, 2002).
5   See *On the Genealogy of Morals*, tr. Douglas Smith (Oxford: Oxford University Press, 1996) p. 39
6   See 'Ulysses Gramophone' in Jacques Derrida, *Acts of Literature*, ed. Derek Attridge (London: Routledge, 1992) p. 287.

CHAPTER 2 VALUE AFTER THEORY: FRANK KERMODE

1   *Poetry, Narrative, History* (Oxford: Blackwell, 1990).
2   See Frank Kermode, *Not Entitled* (London: Flamingo, 1996), p. 219.
3   Frank Kermode, *Shakespeare's Language* (Harmondsworth: Penguin, 2000).
4   Mary Poovey, 'The model system of contemporary literature criticism', *Critical Inquiry* 27 (Spring 2001), 408–38.
5   Louis Althusser, the structuralist Marxist, was arrested in November 1980 for the strangulation murder of his wife; he was declared unfit to plead and confined to psychiatric hospital.
6   Mark Bauerlein, *Literary Criticism: An Autopsy* (Philadelphia, PA: University of Pennsylvania Press, 1997).
7   See 'The discipline of deconstruction', *PMLA* (1992), 1266–79.
8   See Willam Empson, *Argufying* (London: Chatto & Windus, 1987) p. 52.

CHAPTER 3 TRUTH AFTER THEORY: CHRISTOPHER NORRIS

1   Christopher Norris, *Derrida* (London: Fontana), pp. 52–3.

2   Ibid., p. 54.
3   See *Dissemination* [1972] (London: Athlone, 1981) pp. 287–366.

CHAPTER 4   MUSIC, RELIGION AND ART AFTER THEORY: FRANK KERMODE
AND CHRISTOPHER NORRIS

1   'Seeing Salvation: The Image of Christ', Spring 2000.
2   See 'Violence and Metaphysics', in *Writing and Difference* (London: Routledge, 1978), pp. 79–153.

CHAPTER 5   FEMINIST THEORY AFTER THEORY: TORIL MOI

1   For an explanation of Bourdieu's use of *habitus* and 'field' see *What is a Woman?*, pp. 270–1.

EPILOGUE   COMING BACK TO 'LIFE': JOHN SCHAD

1   Quoted in Michael Bell, *F. R. Leavis* (London: Routledge, 1988) p. 110.
2   F. R. Leavis, *Valuation in Criticism and Other Essays* (Cambridge: Cambridge University Press, 1986) p. 287.
3   See Ronald Hayman, *Leavis* (London : Heinemann, 1976) p. 1.
4   See Jacques Derrida, *Points . . . Interviews, 1974-1994*, ed. Elisabeth Weber (Stanford, CA: Stanford University Press, 1992); see Geoff Bennington and Jacques Derrida, *Jacques Derrida* (Chicago, IL: University of Chicago Press, 1993) p. 12.
5   Roland Barthes, *Image-Music-Text*, ed. Stephen Heath (London: Collins, 1977) p. 163.
6   Valentine Cunningham, *Reading after Theory* (Oxford: Blackwell, 2002) pp. 69–71; Derrida performed alongside Ornette Coleman at the 1995 La Villette Jazz Fesitival – see Catherine Malabou and Jacques Derrida, *Jacques Derrida: La Contre-Allée* (Paris: La Quinzaine Littéraire,1999), p. 101.
7   Oscar Wilde, *Plays, Prose Writings and Poems* (London: Everyman, 1996), pp. 99, 105, 124.
8   See F. R. Leavis, *The Critic as Anti-Philosopher*, ed. G.Singh (London: Chatto & Windus, 1982), p. 137.
9   *The Essays of Virginia Woolf*, ed. Andrew McNeillie, 4 vols (London: Hogarth Press, 1994), 4.342–8.
10   Terry Eagleton, *Literary Theory*, 2nd edn (Oxford: Blackwell, 1996), p. 27.
11   See Christopher Norris, *William Empson and the Philosophy of Literary Criticism* (London: Athlone Press, 1978), p. 205. I allude, of course, to Christopher Isherwood's novel, *Mr Norris Changes Trains* (1935).
12   See above, p. 56.

13 T. S. Eliot, *Sacred Wood: Essays on Poetry and Criticism* (London: Methuen, 1960), p. 48.
14 Sigmund Freud, *Beyond the Pleasure Principle*, Penguin Freud Library, 15 vols (London: Penguin, 1984), 11.311; Jacques Derrida, *The Post Card: From Socrates to Freud and Beyond* (Chicago, IL: Chicago University Press, 1987) p. 285.
15 Jacques Derrida, *Glas*, tr. John P. Leavey and Nicholas Rand (Lincoln, NE: Nebraska University Press, 1986) p. 82a.
16 See above, p. 64.
17 *Glas*, pp. 77a, 15b.
18 Derrida, 'Circumfession', p. 213.
19 Wilde, p. 121; Michel Foucault, *The Archaeology of Knowledge*, tr. A.M.Sheridan Smith (London: Routledge, 1972) p. 17; 'L'Intellectuel et les pouvoirs', *La Revue Nouvelle* 80 (October 1984), 339.
20 Derrida, 'Circumfession', p. 311; Jacques Derrida, *Acts of Literature* (London: Routledge, 1992), p. 34.
21 Walter Benjamin, *Illuminations*, tr. Harry Zohn (London: Fontana, 1992), p. 254.
22 Paul de Man, *Blindness and Insight*, 2nd edn (London: Routledge, 1983), p. 55.
23 Jacques Derrida, *Writing and Difference*, tr. Alan Bass (London: Routledge, 1978), p. 292.
24 Terry Eagleton, *The Function of Criticism* (London: Verso, 1984), p. 101.
25 Jacques Derrida, *Spectres of Marx*, tr. Peggy Kamuf (London: Routledge, 1994), p. 14.
26 See William Empson, *Argufying*, ed. John Haffenden (London: Chatto & Windus, 1987), p. 41.
27 John Ayto, *Bloomsbury Dictionary of Word Origins* (London: Bloomsbury, 1991), p. 323.
28 See Catherine Clément, *The Lives and Legends of Jacques Lacan*, tr. Arthur Goldhammer (New York: Columbia University Press, 1983), p. 19; see Althusser, *The Future Lasts a Long Time*, tr. Richard Veasey (London: Chatto & Windus, 1993); quoted in David Macey, *The Lives of Michel Foucault* (London: Vintage, 1993), p. 347.
29 See Jacques Derrida, *The Work of Mourning*, eds Pascale-Anne Brault and Michael Naas (Chicago, IL: Chicago University Press, 2001).
30 Ibid., p. 215.
31 I quote Derrida's lecture from the morning – 'Perjuries', as yet unpublished; Derrida himself here quotes Pierre Fontanier, *Les figures du discours* (Paris Flammarion, 1968) p. 315.
32 Paul de Man, *The Rhetoric of Romanticism* (New York: Columbia University Press,1984), p. 81.
33 See above, p. 28.
34 'Perjuries'.
35 Samuel Taylor Coleridge, *Poetical Works*, ed. Ernest Hartley Coleridge (Oxford: Oxford University Press, 1912), p. 296.
36 Frank Kermode, *Not Entitled: A Memoir* (London: Flamingo, 1995), p. 219.
37 Derrida, *The Post Card*, pp. 127–8; Jacques Lacan, 'A love letter' (1975), in

Juliet Mitchell and Jacqueline Rose (eds), *Feminine Sexuality* (London: Macmillan, 1982), p. 154.
38 For an excellent survey of this development, see Graham Ward, *Theology and Contemporary Critical Theory* (Houndmills: Palgrave, 1999); see also John Schad, 'Hostage of the word: poststructuralism's gospel intertext', *Religion and Literature* 25 (1993), 1–16.
39 Frank Kermode, *Essays on Fiction, 1971–82* (London: Routledge, 1983), p. 31.
40 Frank Kermode, *The Classic* (London: Faber, 1975), p. 138.
41 Frank Kermode, *The Genesis of Secrecy* (Cambridge, MA: Harvard University Press, 1979) p. 14; see *Wordsworth: Poetical Works*, ed. Ernest de Selincourt (Oxford: Oxford University Press, 1936), p. 204; see Stanley E. Fish, *Surprised by Sin* (London: Macmillan, 1967).
42 Jacques Derrida, 'Circumfession', p. 46; Hélène Cixous, *Coming to Writing and Other Essays*, ed. Deborah Johnson (Cambridge, MA: Harvard University Press, 1991), p. 45; Derrida, *The Post Card*, p. 33.
43 See above p. 49.
44 Barthes, *Image-Music-Text*, p. 157.
45 Jacques Derrida, *The Gift of Death*, tr. David Wills (Chicago, IL: Chicago University Press, 1995), p. 69.
46 Sigmund Freud, *Introductory Lectures on Psychoanalysis*, Penguin Freud Library, 15 vols, tr. James Strachey (London: Penguin, 1973), 1.53.
47 See above, p. 31.
48 Kermode, *Essays on Fiction*, pp. 156–67; Derrida, *Acts of Literature*, pp. 36–7.
49 Jean-Paul Sartre, *What is Literature?* tr. Bernard Frechtman (London: Methuen, 1967), p. 45.
50 Jean-Paul Sartre, *Existentialism and Humanism*, tr. Philip Mairet (London: Methuen, 1973), p. 34.
51 See above, p. 4.
52 'Perjuries'.
53 See above, pp. 57–8.
54 Ibid.; Jacques Lacan, *Écrits*, tr. Alan Sheridan (London: Tavistock/Routledge, 1977), p. 166.
55 See *Basic Writings: Martin Heidegger*, ed. David Farrell Krell (London: Routledge, 1993), p. 366.
56 See 'Perjuries'; see Pierre Macherey, *A Theory of Literary Production* (London: Routledge, 1978), p. 94.
57 Michel Foucault, *The Order of Discourse*, in Robert Young (ed.), *Untying the Text* (London: Routledge, 1981), p. 53; Luce Irigaray, *This Sex Which Is Not One*, tr. Catherine Porter (Ithaca, NY: Cornell University Press, 1985); Jacques Lacan, *Écrits*, 2 vols (Paris: Éditions du Seuil, 1977), 1.392.
58 Ferdinand de Saussure, *Course in General Linguistics*, tr. Roy Harris (London: Duckworth, 1983), p. 115; Eagleton, p. 110.
59 Jacques Derrida, 'Letter to a Japanese friend', in Peggy Kamuf (ed.), *A Derrida Reader* (London: Harvester Wheatsheaf, 1991), p. 275.
60 Lacan, *Écrits: A Selection*, pp. 154–5.

NOTES

61 I. A. Richards, *Principles of Literary Criticism* (London: Routledge, 1960), p. 84.
62 Gregory Ulmer, 'The object of post-criticism', in Hal Foster (ed.), *The Anti-Aesthetic: Essays on Postmodern Culture* (Port Townsend, WA: Bay Press, 1983), p. 83.
63 Quoted by Ulmer, ibid., p. 83.
64 Jacques Derrida, *Spurs/Éperons* (Chicago, IL: Chicago University Press, 1979), pp. 122–43.
65 Quoted in Frank Kermode, *The Uses of Error* (London: Collins, 1990), p. 117.
66 Derrida, *The Post Card*, pp. 154, 176.
67 Ibid., p. 32.
68 Søren Kierkegaard, *Fear and Trembling*, tr. Alistair Hannay (Harmondsworth: Penguin, 1985), p. 67.
69 See Terry Eagleton, *Against the Grain, Essays 1975-1985* (London: Verso, 1986), pp. 149–66.
70 Wilde, p. 97.
71 Lacan, *Écrits*, p. 388.
72 Heidegger, *Basic Writings*, p. 389.
73 Hélène Cixous, 'The Laugh of the Medusa', in *New French Feminism*, ed. Elaine Marks and Isabelle de Courtivron (London: Harvester Wheatsheaf, 1981), p. 260.
74 *Post Card*, p. 142.
75 'Perjuries'.
76 Derrida, *Spectres*, p. xviii.
77 Peter Scheckner (ed.), *An Anthology of Chartist Poetry* (London: Associated University Presses, 1989), p. 199.

Index

acolyte 5, 7
Althusser, Louis 65, 173, 176, 180
anacoluthon 5–7, 177–8
anger 14–18
Anidjar, Gil 46–7
Arnold, Matthew 169–70, 188
Aristotle 59, 64, 89
Austin, J. L. 39
autobiography 144, 173

Barthes, Roland 53, 169, 173, 181
bathos 37
Baudrillard, Jean 79, 84
Bauerlin, Mark 66
Beauvoir, Simone de 136, 146–7, 152–54, 163–4
Benjamin, Walter 174
Bennett, Arnold 73
Bloom, Harold 175
Bourdieu, Pierre 153–56
Bowie, Malcolm 53
Brooks, Cleanth 60
Browning, Robert 15
Burke, Kenneth 60
Butler, Judith 150–1

Cage, John 187
Cambridge University 2, 50, 57, 168
Cavell, Stanley 40, 97, 161–3
Christianity 30–1, 33, 35–6, 45–7, 49–50, 124–32, 178–9
Cixous, Hélène 179, 181, 188
Coleridge, Samuel Taylor 178
Critical Inquiry 63
Culler, Jonathan 53, 57
Cunningham, Valentine 169

death 171–2
Descartes, René 184

Derrida, Jacques 56, 80, 82–3, 99–101, 108–13, 154–56, 169, 172–89
Duke University 150
Dummett, Michael 85–6, 88

Eagleton, Terry 171, 175, 184, 187
Empson, William 68–9, 82, 103–7, 123–4
ethics 31–2
existentialism 150–2

Fanon, Frantz 151
Fish, Stanley 79, 180
Fodor, Jerry 122
following 5–10, 14
Fontanier, Pierre 177, 189
forgetting 47
Foucault, Michel 65, 67, 88, 173–4, 176, 180, 184
Frege, G. L. G. 19
Freud, Sigmund 33, 171, 182
friendship 16
Frye, Northrop 59

ghosts 15–18, 34
Ginsburg, Carlo 28
globalisation 163–4
grammar 6, 13
Green, Henry 72
Greene, Graham 72
Gulf War 84

Hartman, Geoffrey 175
Heath, Stephen 57
Hegel, G.W.F. 172
Heidegger, Martin 35, 41, 48, 90–1, 184, 188
Holloway, John 69

Hume, David 24
Husserl, Edmund 41

identity 25–6
Irigaray, Luce 179, 184
Islam 46–7

James, Henry 73
Jameson, Frederic 90
jazz 169
Johnson, Samuel 62
Joyce, James 73–4, 188
Judaism 45–7, 50

Kant, Immanuel 110–12
Kentucky, University of 59–60
Kerman, Joseph 119
Kermode, Frank 170, 171, 172,
    178–80, 182–3
Kierkegaard, Søren 35–6, 113, 130,
    187
Kristeva, Julia 141, 144, 148–9, 179
Kuhn, Thomas S. 89

Lacan, Jacques 176, 179 , 184–6, 188
Lavers, Annette 53
Law, the 29, 42–44
Leavis, F.R. 60 , 74, 168, 170–1, 172,
    175
Levinas, Emmanuel 11, 128
Lévy, Bernard-Henri 151
literariness 19–20, 58, 117, 121
London, University College 53,57, 83
London Review of Books 61, 66
Lyotard, Jean-François 96, 176

MacGregor, Neil 127
Macherey, Pierre 184
Man, Paul de 3–4, 17, 22, 28, 34–5, 40,
    79, 120, 174–5, 177, 186
Marcus, Ruth Bacan 101
marriage 10–11, 30–1
Miller, Hillis J. 22–3, 31
Moi, Toril 183, 188
Montaigne, Michel Eyquem de 5

Nealon, Jeffrey 67
Necessity 8–9, 18
New York Times 158
Nietzsche 47–9, 79
Norris, Christopher 53, 57, 171
Nussbaum, Martha 160–1

organicism 63–4, 76
Other, the 12
Oxford University 138, 187

perjury 4, 11–12, 40–44
pianos 168–70
Poovey, Mary 63
psychoanalysis 43

Raleigh, Walter 170–71
reference 19–21, 26–8
responsibility 49
rhythm 37–8
Richards, I.A. 77, 175 , 186
Rorty, Richard 79, 93–4, 98–9, 116
Rose, Jacqueline 53
Russell, Bertrand 20

Sartre, Jean-Paul 146–7, 151–53, 183
Saussure, Ferdinand de 184–5
Schenker, Heinrich 120
Scott, Joan 149
Searle, John 18, 23, 26–7
secret, the 34
Shakespeare, William 55, 76
signature 10
Smith, Barbara Herrnstein 69
Sokal 94–6, 107–8
Stein, Gertrude 174
surrealism 186

Taylor, Mark C. 131
Thomas, Henri 3–4, 17
Times Literary Supplement 65, 144
Trapp, Joe 71
Trilling, Lionel 61

uncanny, the 32–35
Ulmer, Gregory 186

Valéry, Paul-Ambroise 185

Walker, Perkin 71
war 175–6
Warburg, Aby 70
White, Hayden 28, 79, 87–8, 186
Wilde, Oscar 169, 173, 185, 187
Wittgenstein, Ludwig 54, 79, 113, 145,
    170
woman 6, 12
Woolf, Virginia 135, 170
Wordsworth, William 180

Yates, Frances 71